Endpoint Detection and Response (EDR) Strategies

James Relington

DEDICATION

To those who seek knowledge, inspiration, and new perspectives—
may this book be a companion on your journey, a spark for curiosity,
and a reminder that every page turned is a step toward discovery.

AKNOWLEDGEMENTS

I would like to express my deepest gratitude to everyone who contributed to the creation of this book. To my colleagues and mentors, your insights and expertise have been invaluable. A special thank you to my family and friends for their unwavering support and encouragement throughout this journey.

Understanding the Fundamentals of EDR

Endpoint Detection and Response (EDR) is a cornerstone of modern cybersecurity, designed to provide advanced threat detection, investigation, and response capabilities at the endpoint level. As organizations increasingly rely on distributed computing environments, mobile workforces, and cloud-based operations, traditional perimeter defenses are no longer sufficient. Threat actors have adapted by targeting endpoints, which are often less secure than centralized infrastructure. Laptops, desktops, mobile devices, and servers represent critical entry points into enterprise networks, making endpoint protection more vital than ever. EDR solutions address this need by continuously monitoring endpoint activities and providing tools to detect suspicious behavior, analyze threats, and orchestrate a rapid response to mitigate risks.

At its core, EDR functions as a combination of continuous data collection, real-time analytics, and threat response mechanisms focused on endpoint devices. Unlike traditional antivirus tools that rely heavily on signature-based detection, EDR incorporates behavioral analysis, anomaly detection, and heuristic techniques to identify novel threats and complex attack patterns. This shift allows security teams to uncover threats that would otherwise remain invisible, such as zero-day exploits, fileless malware, and living-off-the-land attacks. By observing behaviors and patterns over time, EDR tools can identify indicators of compromise that may not match any known threat signatures, enhancing the organization's ability to prevent breaches.

One of the defining aspects of EDR is its ability to provide deep visibility into endpoint activities. This includes process execution, file access, registry changes, network connections, and user behaviors. With such detailed telemetry, analysts can reconstruct the full scope of an attack, identifying initial entry points, lateral movement, privilege escalation, and data exfiltration paths. This level of insight is critical for root cause analysis and allows organizations to learn from incidents and improve their defensive posture over time. Furthermore, EDR solutions often include centralized dashboards and investigative tools that help correlate events across multiple endpoints, providing a unified view of the threat landscape.

Detection is only one part of the equation. Equally important is the response component, which allows organizations to contain and remediate threats in real time. EDR platforms typically offer a range of response actions, such as isolating a device from the network, terminating malicious processes, deleting or quarantining files, and initiating forensic investigations. These capabilities are essential for limiting the damage caused by an active threat and for preventing it from spreading further within the environment. By automating certain response actions, EDR systems can also reduce the time between detection and remediation, helping to minimize dwell time and improve overall security outcomes.

The integration of machine learning and artificial intelligence into EDR systems has significantly enhanced their effectiveness. These technologies enable EDR platforms to analyze vast amounts of data quickly and identify patterns that may elude human analysts. For example, machine learning models can detect deviations from normal behavior, such as unusual process launches, unexpected data transfers, or abnormal login patterns. Over time, these models learn what constitutes normal behavior for a particular environment, allowing them to better identify anomalies that may signal an attack in progress. This adaptability makes EDR a dynamic and responsive solution, capable of evolving alongside emerging threats.

EDR is not a standalone solution but rather a component of a broader cybersecurity ecosystem. It often integrates with other tools such as Security Information and Event Management (SIEM) systems, threat intelligence platforms, vulnerability scanners, and network detection solutions. These integrations enhance the contextual awareness of EDR, allowing it to make more informed decisions and contribute to a coordinated defense strategy. For example, alerts generated by EDR can be enriched with external threat intelligence, helping analysts prioritize incidents based on the known severity of a given threat actor or malware family. Similarly, data from EDR can feed into SIEMs to support broader investigations and compliance reporting.

While EDR provides powerful capabilities, it also introduces new challenges. One of the most significant is the management of alerts and false positives. Because EDR systems are designed to detect a wide range of potential threats, they can generate a high volume of alerts, many of which may not be malicious. This can lead to alert fatigue, where analysts become overwhelmed and begin to ignore or overlook important signals. Effective tuning, baselining, and the use of automated triage tools are necessary to reduce noise and ensure that the most critical alerts receive immediate attention. Additionally, organizations must invest in training and staffing to ensure they have the expertise required to operate and interpret EDR tools effectively.

Another challenge is balancing security with performance. Because EDR solutions collect and analyze large volumes of endpoint data, they can impact system performance if not properly optimized. This is particularly important in environments with resource-constrained devices or in scenarios where user experience is critical. Modern EDR platforms strive to minimize their footprint through lightweight agents and efficient data processing techniques, but organizations must still assess the impact on their specific environments during deployment.

EDR is also influenced by legal and regulatory considerations. The collection and storage of endpoint data, especially in industries dealing with sensitive or personal information, must comply with data protection regulations such as GDPR, HIPAA, or PCI-DSS. Organizations need to implement appropriate safeguards to ensure that EDR data is encrypted, access-controlled, and retained in accordance with legal requirements. Transparency about data collection and usage is also important to maintain trust with employees and stakeholders.

As cybersecurity threats become more advanced and persistent, the need for robust endpoint detection and response capabilities will only grow. EDR offers a proactive approach to security, empowering organizations to detect threats earlier, respond faster, and recover more effectively. By understanding the fundamental principles of EDR—its architecture, detection methods, response capabilities, and integration points—security teams can build a strong foundation for endpoint protection. This understanding is essential not only for choosing the right EDR solution but also for developing strategies that align with the organization's unique risk profile, infrastructure, and operational needs.

The Evolution of Endpoint Security

The history of endpoint security is a reflection of how technology, user behavior, and cyber threats have continuously evolved in tandem. In the earliest days of personal computing, security was not a primary concern. Computers were largely standalone systems with limited connectivity, and the threat landscape was relatively simple. Most security risks at the time came from physical access to machines or infected floppy disks. Basic antivirus programs were developed to address these issues by identifying and removing known malicious files based on static signatures. These early solutions were reactive in nature, offering minimal protection against new or unknown threats, but they were sufficient for the relatively low-risk environments of the time.

As computer networks grew in complexity and the internet became more widespread, the nature of threats changed dramatically. Attackers began exploiting the interconnectedness of systems to spread malware at scale, target vulnerabilities in operating systems, and launch attacks from remote locations. Traditional antivirus solutions struggled to keep up, as they relied on frequent signature updates and lacked the ability to detect novel or polymorphic threats. This prompted the development of more sophisticated security tools, such as host-based intrusion detection systems, personal firewalls, and heuristic scanning engines. These advancements marked the beginning of a shift toward more proactive security models that aimed not only to identify known threats but also to detect suspicious behavior and block unknown attacks.

The rise of enterprise networks brought with it a new layer of complexity. Organizations now had to manage and secure thousands of endpoints across geographically dispersed locations. Centralized management became essential, leading to the emergence of endpoint protection platforms that combined antivirus, anti-spyware, firewall, and device control functionalities into a single solution. These platforms introduced the concept of centralized policy enforcement, allowing administrators to maintain control over endpoints from a single console. This consolidation improved operational efficiency and offered a more consistent level of protection, but it also highlighted the limitations of relying on preventive controls alone.

As attackers became more sophisticated, they began using advanced techniques such as social engineering, zero-day exploits, and fileless malware to bypass traditional defenses. The limitations of signature-based detection became increasingly apparent, especially in the face of targeted attacks designed to evade existing controls. Organizations began to realize that no security solution could guarantee complete prevention. This marked a pivotal moment in the evolution of endpoint security: the transition from prevention-focused models to detection and response strategies. Rather than attempting to block every threat outright, security teams needed the ability to detect breaches quickly, investigate incidents, and respond effectively to limit damage.

This need gave rise to the concept of Endpoint Detection and Response (EDR), a significant milestone in the evolution of endpoint security. EDR solutions were built to provide continuous monitoring, behavioral analysis, and real-time response capabilities at the endpoint level. Unlike traditional tools that focused on prevention, EDR acknowledged the inevitability of breaches and focused on minimizing their impact. By collecting and analyzing large volumes of endpoint telemetry, EDR tools enabled organizations to identify subtle indicators of compromise, investigate the full scope of an incident, and take immediate action to contain threats. This approach represented a more dynamic and resilient form of endpoint security, one that embraced visibility, intelligence, and agility.

The growing complexity of the threat landscape, coupled with the increasing reliance on cloud computing and remote workforces, further accelerated the evolution of endpoint security. Modern endpoints are no longer confined to corporate offices or managed networks. Employees access sensitive data from personal devices, public Wi-Fi, and cloud applications, often beyond the reach of traditional security perimeters. This dissolution of the network boundary introduced new challenges that required a fundamentally different approach to security. Solutions such as cloud-delivered endpoint protection, mobile device management, and identity-centric access controls emerged to address these issues, reflecting a broader shift toward a zero trust security model.

Zero trust principles have had a profound impact on the design of endpoint security strategies. Rather than assuming that devices inside the network are trustworthy, zero trust models operate on the premise that every endpoint must be continuously verified and monitored. Endpoint security tools now play a critical role in enforcing these principles by validating device health, monitoring user behavior, and enforcing adaptive access policies. This approach has made endpoint security more dynamic and context-aware, enabling organizations to enforce granular security policies based on real-time risk assessments rather than static rules.

At the same time, the integration of artificial intelligence and machine learning has transformed how endpoint security solutions operate. These technologies allow security systems to detect patterns, learn from data, and adapt to emerging threats without explicit human input. AI-powered endpoint solutions can identify anomalies in user behavior, detect previously unseen malware, and prioritize alerts based on contextual relevance. By reducing the reliance on manual analysis and accelerating response times, AI has helped close the gap between threat detection and mitigation, making endpoint security more proactive and intelligent.

The evolution of endpoint security has also been influenced by the growing emphasis on regulatory compliance and data privacy. Regulations such as GDPR, HIPAA, and CCPA have imposed strict requirements on how organizations manage and protect sensitive data, including on endpoint devices. Security solutions must now provide not only technical protections but also auditing, reporting, and policy enforcement capabilities to support compliance efforts. This has led to the development of integrated platforms that combine threat detection, data loss prevention, encryption, and compliance management into a unified endpoint security solution.

As organizations continue to navigate an ever-changing threat landscape, the role of endpoint security will remain central to their overall defense strategy. From its humble beginnings as a reactive tool for virus removal, endpoint security has evolved into a complex, adaptive system that spans prevention, detection, response, and compliance. Each stage of this evolution reflects a deeper understanding of the threats facing modern organizations and a commitment to building more resilient and responsive security architectures. The journey of endpoint security is far from over, and as new technologies and threats emerge, the tools and strategies that protect our endpoints will continue to evolve in sophistication and scope.

Core Components of EDR Systems

Endpoint Detection and Response (EDR) systems are built upon a complex and interconnected architecture designed to monitor, detect, investigate, and respond to threats at the endpoint level. Each EDR solution, regardless of vendor or implementation, shares a foundational set of components that work together to provide a comprehensive defense mechanism. These components must operate in real time, across a wide variety of environments, and under the pressure of evolving threats. Understanding the core components of an EDR system is essential for appreciating its power and for deploying it effectively within an organization's broader cybersecurity infrastructure.

At the heart of every EDR system is the endpoint agent. This lightweight piece of software is installed directly on endpoint devices such as desktops, laptops, and servers. The agent operates silently in the background, collecting data about system activities, user behaviors, network connections, process executions, file access, and registry changes. It acts as the primary sensor for the EDR platform, capturing detailed telemetry that can later be analyzed to identify potential threats. The agent must be highly efficient, so as not to degrade the performance of the endpoint, while still collecting enough contextual data to support thorough investigation and accurate detection.

Once the data is gathered, it is transmitted to a centralized data store or analysis engine. This component is responsible for aggregating telemetry from all monitored endpoints and storing it in a way that supports fast querying and correlation. The volume of data generated by endpoints can be substantial, so this component must be both scalable and secure. Cloud-based EDR systems often leverage distributed architectures to ensure high availability and elasticity, allowing organizations to scale their visibility as needed. The centralized data repository serves as the historical record of endpoint activities, providing the context necessary for identifying threats that unfold over time or involve multiple steps.

A critical component of the EDR architecture is the analytics engine. This engine applies a combination of predefined rules, heuristic models, and machine learning algorithms to the collected data. Its purpose is to detect suspicious patterns and behaviors that may indicate the presence of malware, unauthorized access, or lateral movement within the network. The analytics engine is where raw telemetry is transformed into actionable intelligence. Sophisticated EDR platforms use behavioral baselining to identify deviations from normal activity, flagging anomalies that may be signs of compromise. Machine learning models trained on vast datasets can identify subtle correlations and anticipate emerging threats, enhancing the platform's ability to detect new or unknown attack techniques.

Another fundamental element of EDR systems is the detection engine. While the analytics engine identifies potentially interesting patterns, the detection engine is responsible for validating these findings against known indicators of compromise, threat intelligence feeds, and predefined detection rules. This engine uses a multi-layered approach to threat identification, including static analysis, dynamic behavior tracking, and contextual evaluation. It must be both precise and adaptive, capable of minimizing false positives while still capturing sophisticated threats. Integration with external threat intelligence sources enhances the detection engine's effectiveness by providing current data on known attack campaigns, malicious IP addresses, domains, and file hashes.

The investigation console is the user interface through which security analysts interact with the EDR system. This console presents alerts, timelines, visualizations, and contextual data that enable analysts to understand what occurred on an endpoint and how it fits into a broader attack sequence. A well-designed console is critical to the usability of the EDR platform. It must present complex information in a digestible format, support advanced search capabilities, and allow pivoting across data points to trace an attacker's movement. The investigation console is where analysts spend most of their time during an incident, and its functionality can significantly influence the speed and accuracy of response.

The response orchestration component is responsible for executing defensive actions in response to detected threats. These actions may include isolating an endpoint from the network, killing malicious processes, deleting suspicious files, and triggering scripts to remediate or contain the threat. This component often includes customizable playbooks or workflows that guide automated responses based on the severity and context of the alert. By automating response tasks, EDR platforms reduce the time between detection and containment, helping to limit the damage caused by fast-moving attacks. Human analysts can still intervene to make decisions, but automation ensures that basic containment actions are not delayed.

Endpoint isolation is a feature that is tightly integrated with the response component. When an endpoint is suspected of being compromised, isolating it from the rest of the network can prevent the attacker from moving laterally or exfiltrating data. The isolation process is typically controlled through the agent, which can restrict network traffic and enforce local controls while still allowing limited communication with the EDR console for analysis and remediation.

This targeted approach enables organizations to maintain investigative control over the compromised endpoint without risking further spread of the threat.

Telemetry enrichment is another essential capability within EDR systems. Collected data on its own can be noisy and lack context, but by enriching this telemetry with additional metadata, threat intelligence, user identity information, and environmental details, the system helps analysts understand the significance of each event. For example, knowing that a process was launched by a domain administrator at 3 a.m. outside normal working hours may elevate the severity of an alert. This contextual awareness is critical in distinguishing benign anomalies from genuine threats.

Policy management and configuration tools are also core to the operation of EDR systems. Administrators must be able to define what behaviors are acceptable, what thresholds trigger alerts, and what actions should be taken under specific circumstances. These tools allow security teams to tailor the EDR platform to their unique operational environment, risk appetite, and compliance requirements. Policies can be set to control agent behavior, alert sensitivity, data retention, and access permissions.

Finally, integration capabilities are a key component of modern EDR systems. In an enterprise setting, EDR must coexist with a broader ecosystem of security tools, including Security Information and Event Management (SIEM) systems, threat intelligence platforms, security orchestration tools, and network detection systems. The ability to exchange data, share alerts, and coordinate actions across these systems enhances the overall effectiveness of the security posture. Open APIs, support for standard data formats, and bi-directional integrations are increasingly necessary features for organizations seeking a unified and responsive defense architecture.

Each of these components plays a vital role in delivering the detection, visibility, and response capabilities that define EDR. Together, they create a system that not only observes what is happening on endpoints but also understands the significance of those events and acts to defend the organization with precision and speed. The strength of an EDR solution lies not in any one component but in the seamless orchestration of all its parts, working together to protect against a constantly changing and highly adaptive threat environment.

EDR vs Traditional Antivirus Solutions

The landscape of endpoint security has undergone a dramatic transformation in recent years, driven by the increasing sophistication of cyber threats and the evolving requirements of organizations in a hyperconnected digital world. At the center of this transformation lies a shift from traditional antivirus solutions to more advanced systems known as Endpoint Detection and Response, or EDR. While both aim to protect endpoints from malicious activities, they are fundamentally different in design, scope, and capability. Understanding the contrast between traditional antivirus and EDR is essential for organizations seeking to adapt their security strategies to modern threats and operational needs.

Traditional antivirus solutions emerged in an era when malware primarily consisted of known viruses and simple malicious programs that followed predictable patterns. These solutions relied heavily on signature-based detection, a method where unique identifiers or fingerprints of known malware are catalogued and used to scan files and processes. When a match is found, the antivirus engine flags the threat and takes remedial action. For many years, this approach was effective, as the volume and diversity of malware were relatively manageable. Regular updates from antivirus vendors ensured that endpoints could defend themselves against the most recently discovered threats, provided those threats had been previously analyzed and catalogued.

However, the limitations of traditional antivirus became apparent as attackers began deploying more dynamic and evasive techniques. Polymorphic malware, which constantly changes its code to avoid detection, and fileless attacks, which execute entirely in memory without leaving a footprint on the disk, rendered signature-based methods increasingly inadequate. In addition, the rise of targeted attacks and advanced persistent threats meant that cybercriminals no longer needed to create widespread outbreaks; instead, they could craft custom payloads that would likely go undetected by traditional defenses. These shifts highlighted the reactive nature of antivirus tools, which could only defend against threats they had already seen and catalogued.

Endpoint Detection and Response was developed to address these gaps. Unlike traditional antivirus, EDR is not limited to scanning files for known signatures. Instead, it continuously monitors endpoint activities, collecting and analyzing data in real time to detect suspicious behavior, unauthorized changes, and other indicators of compromise. This behavioral-based approach enables EDR to identify threats that are unknown, obfuscated, or tailored to bypass conventional defenses. It moves beyond prevention and incorporates advanced capabilities for detection, investigation, and response, acknowledging that some threats will inevitably breach initial defenses and focusing instead on minimizing the impact and duration of those breaches.

The visibility offered by EDR is a major differentiator. Traditional antivirus operates largely in the background, alerting users only when a known threat is detected. EDR, on the other hand, provides security teams with detailed telemetry from every monitored endpoint. This includes information on process creation, network activity, user logins, file modifications, and registry changes. Armed with this data, analysts can reconstruct the sequence of events leading to an incident, identify how the threat entered the system, determine whether it spread to other endpoints, and take appropriate steps to contain and remediate the issue. This level of insight is far beyond the capabilities of traditional antivirus solutions.

Another significant difference lies in the response mechanisms available to each type of solution. When traditional antivirus detects malware, its typical response options include quarantining the file, deleting it, or blocking its execution. While this may be sufficient for isolated and known threats, it falls short in the face of multi-stage attacks or rapidly spreading malware. EDR systems are built with response in mind. They offer a wider array of remediation actions, such as isolating the affected endpoint from the network, terminating malicious processes, rolling back changes made by the attacker, and initiating forensic data capture. These actions can be automated or manually triggered based on predefined playbooks, significantly reducing the time between detection and mitigation.

Integration is another area where EDR surpasses traditional antivirus. Legacy antivirus tools often function as standalone solutions, with limited ability to share information or coordinate actions with other parts of the security infrastructure. EDR platforms are designed to integrate with Security Information and Event Management systems, threat intelligence feeds, vulnerability scanners, and network security tools. This ecosystem-oriented design enhances the effectiveness of the organization's overall security posture by enabling cross-platform data sharing, coordinated response efforts, and centralized monitoring. EDR also supports modern security frameworks such as Zero Trust and MITRE ATT&CK, making it a more suitable choice for organizations seeking to adopt comprehensive, intelligence-driven defense strategies.

The adaptability of EDR is also a key strength. Machine learning and artificial intelligence capabilities built into EDR systems allow them to learn from past incidents and continuously improve their detection accuracy. Over time, EDR platforms can develop a deep understanding of normal behavior across endpoints and quickly flag deviations that may signify malicious activity. Traditional antivirus, by contrast, remains largely static, relying on external updates from the vendor to remain effective. This dependency makes it slower to adapt to novel threats and limits its ability to deal with advanced tactics used by modern adversaries.

Despite their differences, it is important to recognize that traditional antivirus and EDR are not necessarily mutually exclusive. Many modern endpoint protection platforms incorporate elements of both, blending signature-based detection with behavioral analytics, machine learning, and response automation. This hybrid approach allows organizations to maintain a first line of defense against known threats while also preparing for more sophisticated attacks that require deeper analysis and proactive engagement. However, for organizations facing high-risk environments, compliance requirements, or targeted threat actors, relying solely on traditional antivirus is no longer a viable strategy.

Performance and resource usage also play a role in comparing these solutions. Traditional antivirus tools are typically lightweight and designed to have minimal impact on system performance. EDR, due to its constant monitoring and data analysis requirements, may consume more resources, particularly in environments with limited hardware capabilities. Nonetheless, most modern EDR solutions are built with performance optimization in mind and can be configured to balance security needs with operational requirements. This trade-off is often acceptable, given the significantly enhanced protection and visibility that EDR provides.

Ultimately, the shift from traditional antivirus to EDR reflects a broader evolution in cybersecurity thinking. Organizations can no longer rely on reactive, one-size-fits-all solutions in an environment where threats are dynamic, targeted, and increasingly difficult to detect. EDR represents a proactive, intelligence-driven approach that empowers security teams to not only detect and block threats but also understand and respond to them in depth. This paradigm shift marks a fundamental change in how endpoint security is conceived and implemented across industries.

Threat Landscape and Endpoint Vulnerabilities

The threat landscape has grown increasingly complex, dynamic, and dangerous as digital transformation accelerates and organizations expand their dependency on technology. The endpoint, once considered a secondary concern in cybersecurity, has now become a primary target for attackers. As more devices connect to networks— ranging from laptops and desktops to mobile phones, tablets, and Internet of Things devices—the number of attack surfaces has multiplied exponentially. Each endpoint represents a potential entry point for malicious actors, and their vulnerabilities are frequently exploited in campaigns that span from widespread malware outbreaks to highly targeted and persistent attacks. Understanding the modern threat landscape in relation to endpoint vulnerabilities is critical for any organization aiming to protect its assets and ensure operational continuity.

Cyber threats are no longer confined to simplistic viruses or amateur hackers seeking notoriety. Today's adversaries are sophisticated, well-funded, and often operate within organized crime groups or state-sponsored entities. Their motivations range from financial gain and corporate espionage to political disruption and strategic cyber warfare. These attackers employ a diverse array of tactics, techniques, and procedures designed specifically to evade detection, exploit weaknesses, and achieve persistence within target networks. Endpoints are an ideal target because they are dispersed, often inconsistently managed, and in many cases, not subject to the same security scrutiny as centralized systems. Furthermore, they host sensitive data, credentials, and access points that attackers can leverage for lateral movement or privilege escalation.

The vulnerabilities that plague endpoints are both technical and human in nature. On the technical side, endpoints frequently run outdated software, unpatched operating systems, or poorly configured applications. These weaknesses provide direct opportunities for exploitation. Unpatched vulnerabilities are particularly dangerous, as many of them are well-known and have corresponding exploits readily available in public or underground forums. Despite this, organizations often struggle with patch management due to operational constraints, compatibility issues, or limited visibility into their asset inventory. This delay between vulnerability disclosure and remediation creates a window of opportunity for attackers, often referred to as the vulnerability gap.

Endpoints are also vulnerable through third-party software and plugins that expand system functionality but introduce security risks. These components may not receive the same level of attention during security audits and are often overlooked when applying updates. Additionally, endpoint hardware can present vulnerabilities, especially in devices with embedded firmware or legacy components that no longer receive support. The growing use of bring-your-own-device policies exacerbates the situation, as personal devices are unlikely to conform to enterprise security standards, making them an easy target for attackers seeking to establish a foothold within the network.

Human behavior further compounds endpoint risk. Users can be tricked into downloading malicious files, clicking on deceptive links, or providing sensitive credentials through social engineering tactics such as phishing. These techniques continue to be highly effective and require minimal technical effort from attackers. Social engineering remains one of the most common initial access vectors because it exploits trust, distraction, and lack of security awareness among users. Once an endpoint is compromised in this manner, attackers often install remote access tools, keyloggers, or other forms of malware to maintain control and gather intelligence.

Modern threats are also increasingly fileless in nature. Instead of relying on traditional executables that can be scanned and flagged by antivirus tools, attackers now exploit legitimate system tools such as PowerShell, Windows Management Instrumentation, or scripting environments to carry out malicious actions. These tactics blend in with normal administrative behavior and are difficult to detect without behavioral analysis or contextual monitoring. Fileless malware can execute directly in memory, leaving little to no trace on the hard drive, which makes forensic investigation significantly more difficult and detection by signature-based tools almost impossible.

Advanced persistent threats, or APTs, represent another layer of complexity in the threat landscape. These campaigns involve highly skilled attackers who invest time and resources in understanding their targets, identifying weak points, and crafting custom exploits or malware to breach defenses. APTs often begin with a seemingly benign action such as a phishing email or watering hole attack and progress through stealthy lateral movement, privilege escalation, and long-term data exfiltration. Endpoints are frequently the initial target in these campaigns because they offer direct access to users and their behaviors, as well as potentially sensitive information or credentials that can be leveraged later in the attack.

Ransomware has also evolved into one of the most prominent threats to endpoints. Early versions simply encrypted files on the infected device, but modern ransomware variants now include capabilities for data theft, lateral propagation, and even destruction of backups. Ransomware-as-a-service models have further lowered the barrier to entry, allowing individuals with minimal technical knowledge to launch devastating attacks. Endpoints remain the primary delivery vector for ransomware, whether through malicious email attachments, drive-by downloads, or exploitation of remote desktop services. Once deployed, the ransomware can spread rapidly across networked devices, making endpoint visibility and response speed critical to containment.

The increase in remote work has expanded the threat landscape even further. Employees accessing corporate resources from home networks or public Wi-Fi introduce new vectors for attack. These environments are often less secure than enterprise networks, lacking firewalls, segmentation, or endpoint protection tools. Attackers capitalize on this by deploying man-in-the-middle attacks, credential harvesting techniques, or targeting misconfigured virtual private network connections. Remote endpoints also complicate incident response, as security teams may have limited access or control over affected devices, delaying containment and remediation efforts.

Cybercriminals are also targeting endpoints to exfiltrate sensitive data or intellectual property. Endpoints are often where documents are created, edited, or stored before being transferred to more secure environments. This makes them a valuable source of information for attackers seeking to steal proprietary data or trade secrets. Data exfiltration can be conducted through encrypted channels, disguised as legitimate traffic, and may go unnoticed if proper monitoring tools are not in place. Loss of this data can result in regulatory penalties, reputational damage, and competitive disadvantage.

Despite the growing complexity of the threat landscape, many organizations still rely on outdated security models that focus primarily on perimeter defense. This approach fails to account for the reality that threats often originate inside the network or bypass traditional boundaries altogether. As attackers become more adept at identifying and exploiting endpoint weaknesses, the need for robust endpoint protection strategies becomes more urgent. Security must be embedded directly into the endpoints, with continuous monitoring, real-time analytics, and the ability to detect and respond to threats as they occur.

To defend effectively against these threats, organizations must recognize the endpoint as a critical battleground. Protecting it requires more than just antivirus software or firewalls. It demands a comprehensive, adaptive approach that accounts for the full spectrum of vulnerabilities and threat vectors. This includes not only technical defenses but also user education, policy enforcement, and ongoing threat intelligence. Only by embracing this holistic perspective can organizations hope to stay ahead in the ever-evolving contest between defenders and attackers.

Real-Time Threat Detection Techniques

The effectiveness of any endpoint security strategy increasingly depends on its ability to detect threats in real time. As cyberattacks grow more sophisticated and faster in execution, the margin for delay in threat identification becomes narrower. Traditional approaches to threat detection that relied on periodic scanning or batch analysis are no longer sufficient in a world where attacks can unfold and complete within minutes. Real-time threat detection techniques have emerged as the critical frontline defense against these fast-moving threats, enabling organizations to react at the speed of attack. These techniques combine data collection, behavioral analysis, and automated intelligence to detect malicious activity as it happens, rather than after the damage has been done.

At the core of real-time detection is continuous monitoring of endpoint activity. This involves collecting telemetry data from every process, file access, network request, and system change that occurs on an endpoint. Unlike scheduled scans that might only run once or twice per day, real-time monitoring ensures that the security system is always observing and analyzing activities. This constant vigilance is essential because modern malware often operates with incredible speed and stealth. It may encrypt files, establish command-and-control connections, or exfiltrate data within seconds of being executed. By monitoring in real time, security systems are positioned to detect these behaviors before they achieve their full effect.

Behavioral analysis plays a central role in enabling real-time detection. Rather than relying solely on known malware signatures, behavioral analysis evaluates what a process is doing and compares it to established norms or expected behaviors. For instance, a legitimate word processing application launching a PowerShell script or attempting to modify registry keys would be flagged as anomalous behavior, even if the specific action has not been seen before. This approach allows detection of zero-day threats and customized malware that might otherwise bypass signature-based defenses. Machine learning algorithms often enhance behavioral analysis by learning what constitutes normal activity in a given environment and highlighting deviations that may indicate malicious intent.

Another key technique is memory analysis, which focuses on processes running in volatile memory rather than on disk. Many modern attacks, particularly fileless malware, never write anything to disk and instead execute directly in RAM to avoid detection by traditional file-scanning methods. Real-time detection systems must therefore inspect memory for indicators such as reflective DLL injection, shellcode execution, or suspicious memory allocation patterns. Memory scanning tools must operate efficiently and without introducing significant performance overhead, which requires sophisticated engineering and optimization. The ability to detect in-memory threats as they unfold provides a critical advantage in combating stealthy and evasive malware.

Telemetry correlation across endpoints is also a powerful technique for real-time threat detection. A single suspicious event on one device may not be enough to trigger an alert, but when similar patterns are observed across multiple endpoints, it may indicate a coordinated attack or malware propagation. Correlation engines aggregate data from numerous endpoints and identify patterns that suggest a broader campaign. For example, multiple devices attempting to contact the same suspicious IP address, execute similar scripts, or show signs of privilege escalation in a short time window can be correlated to trigger high-confidence alerts. This approach provides a more holistic view of threats that might otherwise be dismissed as isolated anomalies.

Threat intelligence integration further enhances real-time detection capabilities. By feeding real-time data into a constantly updated repository of known indicators of compromise, security systems can immediately flag connections to malicious domains, access to blacklisted files, or the presence of known malicious hashes. Unlike static signature databases, threat intelligence feeds are dynamic and enriched with context, including the threat actor's tactics, techniques, and procedures. When integrated effectively, these feeds allow security tools to respond instantly to emerging threats seen elsewhere in the world, minimizing the exposure window for newly discovered attacks.

Endpoint agents also employ kernel-level monitoring to detect system-level changes and unauthorized activities. These agents operate at a deep level within the operating system to observe attempts to manipulate drivers, escalate privileges, disable security tools, or modify core system files. Since kernel-level attacks often represent an attacker's attempt to gain full control of a system, early detection is crucial. By intercepting these actions in real time, the agent can prevent escalation and provide immediate alerts to analysts. This level of visibility requires careful design to avoid conflicts with legitimate system operations while maintaining high sensitivity to suspicious behavior.

Heuristic and rule-based engines also contribute to real-time threat detection. These systems use predefined logic to identify suspicious actions based on combinations of conditions or behaviors. For example, a rule might flag a script that deletes shadow copies, disables antivirus, and creates a scheduled task for persistence. While not relying on known malware signatures, these rules encapsulate known malicious patterns and allow for swift identification of similar activities. Heuristic engines must be continuously updated and tuned to reflect the latest attack trends and avoid an overwhelming volume of false positives that could desensitize analysts to real threats.

User and entity behavior analytics (UEBA) are increasingly important in real-time detection, especially in environments where insider threats and credential misuse are concerns. UEBA systems establish baselines for how users and devices typically behave and alert when those patterns shift. If a user suddenly accesses large amounts of sensitive data at an unusual time, logs in from a different geographic location, or attempts to disable security controls, the system can respond in real time. This capability is essential for identifying account compromise, lateral movement, and other forms of insider or impersonation-based attacks that bypass traditional perimeter defenses.

Automated response mechanisms are often tightly coupled with real-time detection. Once a threat is identified, the system may immediately isolate the endpoint, terminate the offending process, or block the associated IP address. This automation ensures that damage is contained without waiting for manual intervention. In more advanced systems, these responses are governed by dynamic playbooks that adjust based on the nature of the threat and the environment's risk tolerance. Automation allows security teams to focus on investigation and strategy while ensuring that basic defense actions are carried out within milliseconds of threat detection.

Visualization and alerting dashboards play an important supporting role by providing analysts with real-time insights into what is happening across the environment. These interfaces display threat timelines, process trees, and network maps that help teams quickly understand the scope and origin of an incident. Real-time dashboards must prioritize the most critical threats and provide contextual data to support rapid triage. Without clear and actionable visibility, even the most advanced detection techniques can become lost in a flood of raw data and irrelevant alerts.

Real-time threat detection techniques form the backbone of a modern endpoint security architecture. As attackers continue to innovate and compress the timeline between initial compromise and full impact, security systems must be equipped to respond instantly. Through continuous monitoring, behavioral analysis, memory inspection, correlation, threat intelligence, and automation, real-time detection provides the speed and precision necessary to disrupt attacks before they reach their objectives. By investing in and refining these capabilities, organizations strengthen their ability to withstand the growing tide of cyber threats and reduce the likelihood of successful breaches at the endpoint.

Behavioral Analysis in EDR

Behavioral analysis is one of the most transformative components of modern Endpoint Detection and Response systems, redefining how threats are identified and how organizations protect their critical assets. Unlike traditional methods that focus on known indicators such as file signatures or specific code patterns, behavioral analysis dives deeper into the context and intent of actions occurring on an endpoint. It operates on the principle that malicious behavior, regardless of how it is packaged or delivered, will ultimately reveal itself through anomalous patterns that deviate from normal operations. This capability is especially valuable in today's threat landscape, where attackers increasingly employ sophisticated, stealthy, and adaptive techniques designed to bypass static defenses.

At its core, behavioral analysis involves continuously monitoring the activities of processes, users, and applications to identify patterns that suggest malicious intent. This includes tracking how files are accessed, what scripts are executed, which network connections are established, and how system resources are manipulated. By collecting and analyzing this telemetry in real time, EDR systems can detect subtle signals of compromise that would otherwise go unnoticed. For instance, a benign-looking process might begin encrypting user files, launching obfuscated scripts, or interacting with command and control servers in ways that are inconsistent with its expected behavior. These anomalies, when viewed in the context of broader activity patterns, can raise red flags and trigger alerts for further investigation.

The strength of behavioral analysis lies in its ability to detect unknown, zero-day, and fileless threats. Traditional antivirus tools are limited by their dependence on previously identified malware samples. If a piece of malware has never been seen before, it is unlikely to be caught by signature-based detection. Behavioral analysis, on the other hand, is not constrained by the uniqueness of the malware sample but rather focuses on what that sample does once it is executed. This allows EDR systems to catch attacks that utilize novel code, dynamically generated payloads, or techniques that intentionally avoid matching known indicators. It also enables the detection of fileless malware, which lives entirely in memory and uses legitimate system tools to carry out its malicious goals.

One of the key enablers of effective behavioral analysis is the baseline. EDR systems must understand what constitutes normal behavior within a specific environment in order to identify deviations. This involves establishing behavioral baselines over time, using historical data to define patterns for users, applications, endpoints, and network interactions. Once these baselines are in place, deviations can be measured and evaluated. For example, if an endpoint that typically communicates only with internal services suddenly starts connecting to external IP addresses in a foreign country, this deviation could suggest command and control activity. Similarly, if a user who regularly works during office hours suddenly initiates large data transfers late at night, the behavior may warrant further scrutiny.

Machine learning plays a crucial role in refining these baselines and enhancing the accuracy of behavioral detection. By analyzing large volumes of historical and real-time data, machine learning models can identify patterns that are too complex or subtle for human analysts to detect. These models can continuously adapt to changes in behavior, learning from new data to improve their predictions and reduce false positives. For example, an employee's travel to a new geographic location might initially trigger an alert, but if similar patterns are observed regularly and validated as legitimate, the system can learn to accept them as normal. This adaptability is essential for maintaining both the sensitivity and specificity of behavioral analysis.

Another important dimension of behavioral analysis is context. Isolated behaviors may not always indicate a threat, but when correlated with other events, they can form a clearer picture of malicious activity. Contextual awareness allows EDR systems to differentiate between legitimate administrative actions and suspicious activities. For example, the use of PowerShell to download a script from the internet might be legitimate in certain scenarios, but if it occurs on a user's workstation with no administrative privileges and is followed by the creation of scheduled tasks or registry modifications, the behavior becomes highly suspicious. This contextual analysis helps reduce noise and allows security teams to focus on the most credible threats.

Behavioral analysis is also vital in identifying living-off-the-land attacks, in which attackers use legitimate system tools and processes to achieve their objectives. These techniques are particularly challenging to detect using conventional methods because they do not involve external binaries or malicious files. Instead, they rely on trusted tools like Windows Management Instrumentation, command-line utilities, or scripting languages. Behavioral analysis can expose these techniques by identifying unusual usage patterns or sequences of actions that deviate from the expected norms. Detecting this kind of misuse requires a nuanced understanding of how legitimate tools are normally used within a given environment.

Incident response and investigation benefit significantly from behavioral analysis. When an alert is generated based on behavioral anomalies, the EDR system can present a timeline of related activities that provides investigators with a clear picture of what happened before, during, and after the suspicious event. This timeline allows analysts to trace the attack path, identify affected systems, and understand the scope of the breach. Behavioral data enriches this analysis by offering insights that go beyond the surface level, such as identifying which accounts were used, what files were accessed, or whether data was exfiltrated. This level of detail is crucial for effective containment, remediation, and post-incident forensics.

The impact of behavioral analysis extends to compliance and regulatory reporting as well. Organizations subject to data protection regulations must demonstrate their ability to detect and respond to unauthorized access or data breaches. Behavioral detection provides a strong evidentiary trail that supports compliance efforts, showing that the organization has mechanisms in place to monitor and react to anomalous behavior. It also supports risk management initiatives by highlighting areas of unusual activity that may indicate insider threats or policy violations, allowing organizations to address potential risks before they escalate.

As threats continue to evolve and adapt to traditional defenses, the role of behavioral analysis within EDR will only become more critical. Attackers are increasingly blending in with normal system activity, leveraging legitimate credentials and tools to achieve their objectives without triggering conventional alarms. Behavioral analysis cuts through this camouflage by focusing on what actions are being taken, rather than who is taking them or what tools they are using. It provides a deeper level of visibility into endpoint activities, helping organizations uncover hidden threats and take swift, informed action. By investing in behavioral detection capabilities, security teams can stay one step ahead of adversaries and maintain control over an increasingly complex and dynamic threat environment.

Signature-Based vs Heuristic Detection

The ongoing battle between cyber defenders and malicious actors has led to the development of a wide variety of detection mechanisms, each aimed at identifying threats before they can cause damage. Among these mechanisms, signature-based detection and heuristic detection stand out as two of the most prevalent approaches used in endpoint security, particularly within Endpoint Detection and Response systems. While both methods share the common goal of threat identification, they differ significantly in their techniques, effectiveness, and adaptability to modern threats. Understanding the strengths and limitations of each approach provides insight into how they complement one another and why organizations must often employ both in tandem to achieve comprehensive protection.

Signature-based detection is one of the oldest and most established techniques in cybersecurity. It operates by identifying known threats through unique fingerprints or signatures that are extracted from malicious files, code segments, or behaviors. These signatures are created by analyzing malware samples and documenting patterns such as specific byte sequences, file hashes, filenames, or command strings. When an endpoint security tool scans a file or monitors activity, it compares what it finds against this database of known signatures. If a match is found, the object is flagged as malicious and blocked or quarantined depending on the policy in place. This method is highly effective against well-documented malware families and has historically formed the backbone of traditional antivirus solutions.

The efficiency of signature-based detection lies in its precision and speed. Since it relies on exact matches, the system can quickly and definitively identify threats with minimal processing power. This allows for real-time protection with low false positive rates in environments where known threats are the primary concern. However, the reliance on prior knowledge is also its greatest weakness. Signature-based detection is inherently reactive. It can only detect what it already knows, which means it fails to identify new, unknown, or mutated threats that do not match existing signatures. As threat actors increasingly employ polymorphic malware, which alters its code structure with each infection, the effectiveness of signature-based detection diminishes significantly.

Heuristic detection was developed to overcome the limitations of signature-based approaches by focusing on behaviors and characteristics rather than static patterns. Instead of looking for an exact match to a known threat, heuristic detection evaluates the attributes and behaviors of files and processes to determine whether they exhibit suspicious or malicious tendencies. This method uses rules and algorithms to analyze how a program behaves once it is executed or loaded into memory. For example, if a program attempts to modify critical system files, communicate with known malicious domains, or disguise its process name, the heuristic engine may flag it as potentially harmful even if it has never been seen before.

One of the primary advantages of heuristic detection is its ability to detect zero-day threats and new variants of existing malware. Because it does not depend on predefined signatures, it can identify malware based on behavior alone, making it more flexible and adaptive. This is particularly important in the modern threat landscape where attackers constantly innovate to evade traditional detection methods. Heuristic detection provides a critical layer of defense against advanced persistent threats, fileless attacks, and rapidly evolving malware families. However, this flexibility comes with trade-offs. Heuristic engines are more prone to false positives since legitimate applications can sometimes behave in ways that appear suspicious to the detection algorithms. As a result, careful tuning and contextual awareness are necessary to ensure accurate detection without overwhelming security teams with benign alerts.

To increase their effectiveness, modern heuristic engines often incorporate elements of machine learning and artificial intelligence. By analyzing large datasets of both benign and malicious behaviors, these systems can learn to distinguish subtle differences and improve detection accuracy over time. They can also adjust their decision-making models based on feedback, reducing the likelihood of false positives and enabling more refined threat classification. This dynamic learning capability makes heuristic detection increasingly valuable in environments where threat actors are actively attempting to blend in with normal activity or where custom malware is deployed to bypass signature-based defenses.

Despite their differences, signature-based and heuristic detection methods are not mutually exclusive. In fact, most modern EDR platforms integrate both approaches into a unified detection strategy. Signature-based detection handles the rapid identification and neutralization of known threats, offering high-speed protection against a wide range of common malware. Heuristic detection adds depth by identifying unknown threats, suspicious behaviors, and emerging attack techniques that may not yet have documented signatures. By layering these techniques, organizations can achieve both breadth and depth in their threat detection capabilities, ensuring that neither known nor novel threats slip through the cracks.

Another important consideration is the operational context in which each detection method is applied. In environments with stringent performance requirements, such as those involving legacy systems or low-power devices, signature-based detection may be preferred due to its efficiency and low resource consumption. Conversely, in high-security environments where the risk of targeted attacks is elevated, heuristic detection becomes indispensable despite its heavier processing demands. The decision to emphasize one approach over the other often depends on the organization's risk profile, compliance requirements, and available resources.

The ongoing evolution of cyber threats continues to push detection technologies to adapt and improve. Attackers frequently design malware specifically to evade detection mechanisms, employing obfuscation, encryption, and legitimate tools in their attack chains. This forces security solutions to become more intelligent, contextual, and integrated. While signature-based detection provides a necessary foundation, it is increasingly viewed as a starting point rather than a complete solution. The sophistication of current threats demands the predictive and analytical capabilities of heuristic detection, especially when integrated with broader context from threat intelligence and user behavior analytics.

Organizations that rely solely on signature-based detection risk falling behind the curve, especially in the face of fast-moving and stealthy threats. However, depending only on heuristic detection without the anchor of known indicators can lead to inefficiencies and an overwhelming volume of false alarms. The key lies in the strategic blending of both methods, supported by automation and human oversight. Security professionals must understand how to interpret heuristic findings, validate alerts, and fine-tune detection policies to suit the unique characteristics of their operational environment.

The balance between precision and adaptability is essential in endpoint security. Signature-based detection offers clarity and speed, while heuristic detection delivers flexibility and foresight. Together, they form a complementary defense-in-depth strategy that enhances the organization's ability to identify, contain, and respond to threats in a timely and effective manner. As cyber threats continue to evolve in complexity and frequency, the role of these detection mechanisms will remain central to any comprehensive security architecture, making their integration and refinement a critical task for security teams worldwide.

Endpoint Telemetry and Data Collection

In the realm of modern cybersecurity, visibility is everything. Organizations can only defend what they can see, and in the case of endpoint security, that visibility begins with comprehensive telemetry and data collection. Endpoint telemetry refers to the detailed, ongoing monitoring and logging of activities occurring on endpoint devices, including laptops, desktops, servers, and mobile systems. This data forms the foundational layer upon which detection, investigation, and response capabilities are built in Endpoint Detection and Response systems. The quality, depth, and timeliness of telemetry determine how effectively threats can be identified and how quickly security teams can respond. Without robust data collection, even the most sophisticated detection algorithms and analytics engines are rendered blind to emerging threats.

The process of collecting telemetry begins at the endpoint level through an agent, a lightweight software component that operates in the background of each device. This agent serves as the primary sensor, continuously observing system behavior and capturing events of interest. These events can include process launches, file modifications, registry changes, user logins, network communications, peripheral device activity, and interactions with operating system components. The goal is to create a detailed and time-sequenced narrative of everything happening on the endpoint, which can later be used to detect anomalies, reconstruct attack paths, and conduct forensic analysis. The richness and granularity of this telemetry are critical for the accuracy of threat detection and the precision of response actions.

To be effective, telemetry must be collected in real time and with minimal performance impact on the endpoint. Agents are designed to be lightweight and efficient, filtering and prioritizing the most relevant data points for transmission to a centralized analysis platform. In many cases, raw telemetry is pre-processed at the endpoint to reduce data volume and to apply initial enrichment, such as tagging processes with parent-child relationships or identifying known file hashes. This preprocessing allows the system to preserve context while optimizing bandwidth and storage. Modern EDR systems must balance the need for comprehensive visibility with the constraints of endpoint resources and network performance.

Once collected, telemetry data is transmitted to a central repository or cloud platform where it is stored, analyzed, and correlated. This centralized data lake allows for retrospective investigation, long-term threat hunting, and the application of advanced analytics. Having a historical record of endpoint activity is particularly valuable in detecting threats that unfold over time or involve multiple stages of execution. Attackers often employ tactics that are individually benign but collectively form a pattern of compromise. For example, an attacker may first perform reconnaissance, then establish persistence, and finally exfiltrate data. By storing and analyzing endpoint telemetry over time, EDR systems can connect the dots between seemingly unrelated events and surface them as a coherent threat.

The types of data collected during telemetry are extensive and diverse. Process information includes executable names, command-line arguments, execution timestamps, parent process IDs, and associated file paths. File telemetry captures changes to files, including creation, modification, deletion, and movement, along with associated hashes and metadata. Registry telemetry logs access to critical registry keys, changes to autorun entries, and modifications to system configuration. User activity includes login and logout events, privilege escalations, authentication attempts, and session durations. Network telemetry provides insights into outbound and inbound connections, DNS queries, and data transfers, including unusual communication with external hosts. Each of these data types offers a different piece of the puzzle in understanding endpoint behavior.

Telemetry alone is not enough. To make it actionable, it must be enriched with context and intelligence. Enrichment involves adding metadata such as threat intelligence indicators, geolocation, user roles, system baselines, and historical behavior patterns. For example, knowing that a process is communicating with a foreign IP address flagged by threat intelligence sources greatly increases its risk score. Similarly, if a process is attempting to access system files outside its normal behavior pattern, that anomaly becomes more meaningful when viewed in the context of previous activity. Enriched telemetry enables more accurate detection and prioritization, reducing false positives and helping analysts focus on the most credible threats.

The volume of telemetry data generated across an enterprise can be enormous, especially in environments with thousands of endpoints. Efficient data collection and storage strategies are necessary to manage this scale. Some EDR platforms use compression, deduplication, and intelligent sampling techniques to reduce the data footprint without sacrificing important signals. Others implement tiered storage models, where high-value or recent data is kept in fast-access storage, while less critical or older data is archived for later retrieval. The challenge lies in maintaining high fidelity and responsiveness without overwhelming storage infrastructure or incurring excessive operational costs.

Privacy and compliance considerations also play a significant role in how endpoint telemetry is collected and managed. Because telemetry may include sensitive information such as user actions, file names, and authentication data, organizations must implement strict access controls, data encryption, and retention policies. Compliance with regulations such as GDPR, HIPAA, and CCPA requires transparency in how data is collected, processed, and stored. Organizations must also ensure that telemetry is only used for security purposes and that it does not inadvertently expose confidential or personally identifiable information. Balancing security visibility with user privacy is a delicate but essential responsibility.

The value of telemetry extends beyond detection to enable faster and more effective response. When an incident is detected, having a detailed record of all activities on the affected endpoint allows responders to understand the scope and timeline of the attack. This accelerates containment by identifying which files were altered, which users were involved, what commands were executed, and whether the threat moved laterally to other systems. Telemetry also supports automated response actions, such as rolling back unauthorized changes, quarantining files, or isolating compromised endpoints. Without this data, response efforts are slower, less precise, and more likely to miss hidden components of the attack.

Continuous improvement of detection models also relies heavily on telemetry. Machine learning algorithms use historical data to train and refine their ability to distinguish between normal and malicious behavior. Telemetry serves as the raw input for these models, providing the real-world examples necessary to build effective classifiers and detection rules. As new threats emerge, the system learns from new telemetry to adapt and evolve, ensuring that detection remains effective in the face of changing attacker techniques. This feedback loop between telemetry, detection, and learning is a key driver of resilience in modern endpoint security systems.

Endpoint telemetry and data collection represent the eyes and ears of EDR. Without them, organizations are left navigating threats blindly. With them, security teams gain the insight, context, and evidence needed to detect, investigate, and respond to threats with confidence. As attackers continue to innovate and adapt, the importance of rich, real-time telemetry will only increase. It empowers defenders not just to react to threats, but to anticipate and prevent them, ensuring a more secure and controlled computing environment.

Role of Machine Learning in EDR

Machine learning has fundamentally transformed the landscape of endpoint detection and response by enabling more intelligent, adaptive, and scalable security capabilities. As cyber threats grow in volume, variety, and sophistication, traditional rule-based and signature-driven security models have proven inadequate in providing the agility and depth required for effective defense. Endpoint Detection and Response systems must not only detect known threats but also identify novel and previously unseen attacks that evolve in real time. This challenge requires a level of computational speed, analytical depth, and contextual awareness that only machine learning can provide. By leveraging machine learning models, EDR platforms can process massive volumes of data, recognize complex patterns, and make rapid decisions that significantly enhance threat detection, investigation, and response.

One of the primary contributions of machine learning in EDR is its ability to improve detection accuracy by analyzing endpoint behavior in real time. Unlike traditional approaches that rely solely on static indicators, machine learning models are trained on vast datasets of both benign and malicious activities. These models learn to distinguish normal behavior from anomalous behavior based on thousands of features, including system calls, file operations, network communications, and user actions. Once deployed, the models can identify subtle deviations from established baselines that may indicate the presence of a threat. For example, a model may detect that a process is behaving differently than usual, accessing sensitive files, creating hidden directories, or launching child processes that are not typical for that application. These anomalies, when analyzed within the context of learned behaviors, can trigger high-confidence alerts even when the threat is unknown or obfuscated.

Machine learning also plays a crucial role in reducing false positives, which are a significant challenge in any security monitoring system. High volumes of inaccurate alerts can overwhelm security teams and reduce trust in the system. By continuously refining their understanding of what constitutes normal behavior, machine learning algorithms can better differentiate between legitimate and suspicious activity. Supervised learning techniques, where models are trained with labeled examples of known threats and safe behavior, help improve classification accuracy. Over time, these models adapt to the unique characteristics of each organization's environment, learning what is typical for specific users, applications, and devices. This contextual learning allows the system to filter out noise and focus on genuinely suspicious behavior, freeing analysts to concentrate on the most relevant and dangerous threats.

An important advantage of machine learning is its scalability and speed in processing telemetry data across thousands of endpoints. In large enterprise environments, the sheer volume of data generated by endpoints makes manual analysis or purely rule-based approaches impractical. Machine learning models can ingest, process, and analyze this data at scale, identifying patterns and correlations that would be impossible for human analysts to detect in a timely manner. These models can operate in near real time, flagging threats within seconds and enabling rapid response. This scalability ensures that as organizations grow and the number of endpoints increases, the EDR system remains effective and responsive without compromising detection quality.

Machine learning also enables predictive analytics, allowing EDR platforms to anticipate threats before they fully materialize. By analyzing trends and correlations in historical data, models can identify indicators of emerging attack patterns. For instance, if a combination of seemingly benign behaviors consistently precedes a ransomware infection, the system can learn to recognize this pre-infection behavior and issue alerts early in the attack chain. Predictive capabilities allow for proactive defense measures such as isolation, access restriction, or policy enforcement before significant damage occurs. This shift from reactive to proactive security is a direct result of machine learning's ability to uncover relationships and sequences that are not explicitly defined in rule sets.

In addition to detection, machine learning enhances incident investigation and threat hunting. Models can cluster similar alerts, identify relationships between events, and automatically map activities to known attack frameworks such as MITRE ATT&CK. This correlation helps analysts understand the scope and progression of an attack, identify lateral movement, and prioritize response actions. Unsupervised learning techniques are particularly useful for clustering events and detecting outliers without requiring labeled data. These models can identify previously unknown attack vectors or tactics by grouping together activities that share similar characteristics but have not yet been classified. By accelerating the investigative process and surfacing meaningful insights, machine learning empowers analysts to make informed decisions quickly and effectively.

Another critical role of machine learning in EDR is in automating response actions. When a threat is detected, the system must decide how to react, whether by isolating the endpoint, killing a process, or alerting an analyst. Reinforcement learning and decision-tree models can be employed to evaluate the best response based on previous outcomes and risk assessments. Over time, the system learns which actions are most effective at containing threats without disrupting legitimate activities. This automated decision-making capability helps reduce response times and limit the damage caused by active threats. It also ensures consistency in response actions, which is essential for maintaining compliance and operational continuity.

Machine learning also contributes to the ongoing evolution of EDR platforms through feedback loops. When analysts review and label alerts, their decisions can be fed back into the model to refine its learning. This process, known as active learning, enables the system to continuously improve based on real-world usage and human expertise. By integrating analyst feedback, the models become more accurate, more aligned with organizational policies, and better equipped to handle evolving threat landscapes. This collaborative interaction between human analysts and machine intelligence is a cornerstone of adaptive security and a key factor in the long-term success of EDR solutions.

While the benefits of machine learning in EDR are substantial, there are also challenges that must be addressed. Model transparency and interpretability remain concerns, especially in high-stakes environments where security decisions must be explained and justified. Black-box models that make decisions without clear reasoning can create uncertainty and hinder adoption. To address this, many EDR platforms incorporate explainable AI techniques, providing analysts with insights into why a particular behavior was flagged and how the decision was reached. These explanations not only improve trust in the system but also support training, auditing, and compliance efforts.

Finally, the effectiveness of machine learning in EDR depends heavily on the quality and diversity of the data used to train the models. Bias, imbalance, or lack of representation in the training data can lead to poor performance and blind spots. Continuous data collection, validation, and retraining are necessary to ensure that models remain accurate and relevant in the face of changing threats. Organizations must also be aware of adversarial techniques designed to fool machine learning systems, such as poisoning training data or crafting inputs that evade detection. Building resilient, robust models that can withstand these tactics is an ongoing area of research and innovation in the field of cybersecurity.

The integration of machine learning into EDR systems represents a significant advancement in the fight against cyber threats. It enhances visibility, accelerates detection, improves accuracy, and enables proactive defense strategies that are essential for securing today's complex and dynamic digital environments. As machine learning technology continues to evolve, its role in EDR will only grow more central, driving new capabilities and reshaping the way organizations defend their endpoints against a relentless and ever-changing threat landscape.

Managing False Positives in Detection

False positives are one of the most persistent and challenging issues in cybersecurity, particularly within Endpoint Detection and Response systems. As the volume and complexity of data generated by endpoints increases, so too does the potential for security solutions to misidentify legitimate activity as malicious. A false positive occurs when a system incorrectly flags a harmless action or file as a threat. While this may seem less dangerous than failing to detect an actual threat, the consequences of frequent false positives can be severe. They consume valuable analyst time, erode confidence in the system, delay incident response, and, in the worst cases, cause operational disruptions if legitimate processes are mistakenly blocked or quarantined.

The issue begins with the core design of detection systems, which must constantly strike a delicate balance between sensitivity and specificity. High sensitivity ensures that even subtle or rare indicators of compromise are detected, but this often results in a higher number of false alerts. High specificity reduces false positives but runs the risk of missing true threats. In practice, finding the perfect balance is difficult, particularly in dynamic environments where legitimate behavior can vary widely between users, departments, and devices. For instance, an action that is abnormal in one context may be entirely normal in another, depending on the user role, the system configuration, or the software being used. Without sufficient context, detection systems can misinterpret these variations as signs of malicious activity.

The impact of false positives becomes more significant in large-scale environments where hundreds or thousands of endpoints are monitored simultaneously. A small percentage of false alerts per endpoint can quickly scale into an overwhelming flood of notifications for security analysts. This alert fatigue leads to critical issues being overlooked or delayed as teams struggle to keep up with the volume. Analysts may become desensitized to alerts, developing a habit of dismissing them without proper investigation. This creates a dangerous situation where real threats might be ignored due to the high background noise of benign alerts. Over time, false positives not only waste resources but also degrade the overall security posture by undermining the efficiency and credibility of the detection system.

Managing false positives effectively requires a combination of strategic planning, advanced technology, and continuous tuning of detection mechanisms. One foundational step is the proper baselining of normal activity. By establishing what constitutes typical behavior for each endpoint, user, and application, EDR systems can better distinguish between expected and suspicious actions. This involves observing activity over time and generating behavioral models that reflect the operational norms of the environment. The more accurate and detailed these baselines are, the more effectively the system can identify deviations that truly warrant attention. However, baselining is not a one-time event. It must be continuously updated to reflect changes in usage patterns, software deployments, and organizational workflows.

Machine learning plays an essential role in managing false positives by enabling detection systems to learn and adapt over time. Supervised models trained on labeled datasets can become increasingly accurate in classifying threats versus non-threats. These models benefit from feedback loops, where the decisions of human analysts are used to refine the system's understanding of what should and should not be flagged. This collaborative process helps reduce false positives while maintaining high detection accuracy. Additionally, unsupervised models can identify new patterns without prior labeling, flagging truly novel threats while discarding anomalies that are consistent with known safe behaviors. The key is to provide the system with high-quality, representative data that captures the diversity of the environment.

Another effective technique is contextual enrichment. Alerts generated by the detection engine can be enriched with information from other sources, such as identity management systems, asset inventories, network telemetry, and threat intelligence feeds. By adding this context, the system can make more informed decisions about whether an activity is genuinely suspicious. For example, a script executed by a trusted system administrator during scheduled maintenance should not be treated the same as an identical script launched by a regular user at an unusual hour. Context-aware detection rules can drastically reduce the number of false positives by accounting for who performed the action, when it occurred, what the surrounding circumstances were, and how it aligns with broader patterns of behavior.

Customization and tuning of detection rules are also vital for managing false positives. Out-of-the-box detection templates provided by EDR vendors are often too generic to suit the specific needs of every organization. Security teams must review, adjust, and create rules based on their unique risk profile, threat landscape, and operational environment. This tuning process requires ongoing assessment and testing, where detection thresholds are adjusted, rules are refined, and exceptions are added for known safe behaviors. A well-tuned EDR system should align closely with the organization's real-world activities, minimizing noise without compromising visibility into genuine threats.

The human element plays a critical role as well. Analysts must be trained not only in how to respond to alerts but also in how to identify patterns of false positives and provide feedback to improve detection logic. Collaboration between security teams and IT operations is crucial to understanding the root causes of false alerts and implementing systemic changes that reduce their frequency. For example, if a particular software update consistently triggers false alarms, it may be necessary to whitelist certain actions or adjust the rules governing process behavior. These refinements require clear communication channels, robust documentation, and a culture of continuous improvement.

Automation can help manage false positives at scale by triaging alerts based on severity, confidence, and potential impact. Automated workflows can suppress low-confidence alerts, group related events, or apply predefined responses to known benign triggers. This allows analysts to focus their attention on high-priority incidents that require human judgment and intervention. Over time, as the system learns from outcomes and feedback, these automated processes become more accurate and effective. Automation does not eliminate the need for human oversight, but it enables security teams to operate more efficiently and avoid being overwhelmed by unnecessary alerts.

Ultimately, reducing false positives is an ongoing journey that evolves alongside the organization and the threat landscape. It demands a multifaceted approach that combines technology, process, and people to ensure that detection systems remain both accurate and trustworthy. By investing in adaptive learning, contextual awareness, continuous tuning, and strong operational collaboration, organizations can significantly reduce the burden of false positives. This not only improves security outcomes but also enhances the overall efficiency and morale of the security operations team. An EDR system that delivers high-fidelity alerts without unnecessary noise becomes a powerful ally in the ongoing effort to protect critical assets and maintain operational integrity.

Response Automation and Orchestration

The growing complexity and speed of cyber threats have made it increasingly difficult for human analysts alone to manage detection and response activities in modern security environments. As attackers adopt more sophisticated tactics and reduce the time between initial compromise and full exploitation, organizations need faster, more coordinated, and more consistent ways to react to incidents. This has led to the rise of response automation and orchestration within Endpoint Detection and Response systems. These capabilities serve to enhance the efficiency and effectiveness of security operations by reducing manual intervention, standardizing responses, and integrating diverse tools into a cohesive defensive strategy. Response automation and orchestration are no longer optional luxuries but essential components of a modern endpoint security posture.

Automation in the context of EDR refers to the use of pre-defined rules, scripts, or workflows to carry out specific actions automatically once a threat is detected. These actions can range from simple tasks such as sending an alert or logging an event to more complex responses like isolating an endpoint, terminating malicious processes, or initiating forensic data collection. The speed at which automated responses occur is one of their most critical benefits. In the early stages of an attack, every second counts. By automating key parts of the response, organizations can reduce dwell time, limit the attacker's ability to move laterally, and contain the impact before it escalates into a major breach.

Automation also ensures consistency in how incidents are handled. Human analysts, no matter how experienced, can make inconsistent decisions under pressure, especially when dealing with large volumes of alerts or during high-stress situations. Automated responses, by contrast, follow defined playbooks that are carefully designed and tested in advance. These playbooks specify exactly what actions should be taken under various conditions, eliminating ambiguity and ensuring that every incident is handled in accordance with organizational policies and regulatory requirements. This level of consistency not only improves security outcomes but also supports auditing and compliance efforts by creating a documented record of actions taken.

Orchestration extends the concept of automation by coordinating actions across multiple systems and tools within the security ecosystem. While automation handles the execution of individual tasks, orchestration manages the sequence and integration of those tasks across different domains. For example, when an endpoint threat is detected, an orchestrated response might involve updating firewall rules, revoking access tokens, informing the incident response team, triggering a scan on related systems, and opening a case in the organization's ticketing system. Each of these steps may be executed by a different tool or platform, but orchestration ties them together into a unified, automated workflow. This approach allows organizations to respond to incidents holistically rather than in isolated silos.

Effective orchestration requires deep integration between the EDR system and other components of the security stack, including Security Information and Event Management platforms, threat intelligence feeds, vulnerability scanners, access management systems, and cloud security tools. These integrations enable data sharing and synchronized actions, which are essential for comprehensive threat mitigation. For instance, an EDR platform might receive an alert about suspicious activity, enrich it with threat intelligence from a third-party feed, correlate it with logs from the SIEM, and then trigger a network quarantine through a firewall or NAC solution. Each step amplifies the others, resulting in a faster, smarter, and more coordinated defense.

An important element of automation and orchestration is decision-making logic. Not all threats warrant the same response, and not all environments are equally tolerant of automated actions. For this reason, response workflows often incorporate conditional logic that evaluates the context of the alert before deciding what action to take. Factors such as the confidence level of the detection, the sensitivity of the affected asset, user privileges, and the presence of lateral movement indicators can influence whether the response is fully automated or requires human approval. Some organizations may opt for a hybrid approach, where automation handles the initial stages of response and then hands off control to human analysts for more nuanced decision-making. This flexibility allows organizations to tailor their automation strategies to their risk tolerance and operational maturity.

The benefits of automation and orchestration are not limited to technical outcomes. They also have a significant impact on the efficiency and morale of security teams. By automating routine and repetitive tasks, analysts are freed from alert fatigue and can focus on high-value activities such as threat hunting, investigation, and strategic planning. This not only improves job satisfaction but also enhances the team's ability to detect and respond to advanced threats. Furthermore, automation reduces reliance on individual expertise, making security operations more resilient to personnel changes and ensuring continuity even during staffing shortages or crises.

Developing effective response automation and orchestration strategies requires careful planning, including the identification of use cases, the creation of standardized playbooks, and rigorous testing. It is important to prioritize use cases that are high-impact, high-frequency, or highly time-sensitive. Common scenarios include ransomware containment, privilege misuse, unauthorized application execution, and external command-and-control communication. Each playbook should be designed to achieve specific goals with measurable outcomes, such as reducing mean time to detect, mean time to respond, or the number of endpoints affected. Testing and simulation exercises can help validate these playbooks, identify gaps, and refine workflows before they are deployed in a live environment.

Security teams must also consider the governance of automated response. Clear policies should be in place to define which actions can be automated, under what conditions, and who has the authority to modify or disable automation. Transparency and oversight are critical to maintaining trust in the system and ensuring that automation does not introduce unintended consequences. For example, automatically isolating an endpoint may contain a threat, but it may also disrupt critical business operations if done without proper context or communication. Governance structures, change control processes, and approval workflows help manage these risks and align automation with broader organizational objectives.

As attackers become faster, more persistent, and more creative, the traditional model of manual, reactive incident response is no longer sufficient. Automation and orchestration provide the speed, consistency, and scalability needed to keep pace with modern threats.

They enable organizations to respond to incidents not just with technical precision, but with strategic coherence, drawing on the full capabilities of their security infrastructure in a synchronized and intelligent manner. This transformation allows security operations to move from a reactive stance to a proactive, preventative, and adaptive model, in which threats are anticipated, contained, and neutralized with speed and efficiency. As EDR platforms continue to evolve, the role of automation and orchestration will only grow more central, empowering organizations to protect their environments with greater confidence and control.

Integration of EDR with SIEM Platforms

The integration of Endpoint Detection and Response systems with Security Information and Event Management platforms represents one of the most strategic alliances in modern cybersecurity architecture. While EDR solutions specialize in detecting and responding to threats at the endpoint level, SIEM platforms are designed to aggregate, correlate, and analyze security data from across an entire organization's infrastructure. When these two systems are integrated, the result is a more holistic and coordinated approach to threat detection, investigation, and response. Each platform brings unique strengths, and their collaboration offers security teams broader visibility, richer context, and more intelligent automation capabilities. In an era of increasingly complex and persistent cyber threats, such integration is essential for organizations seeking to maintain a proactive and resilient security posture.

EDR platforms are deeply embedded within endpoint devices, continuously monitoring activity such as process execution, file modifications, registry changes, user interactions, and network connections. This telemetry provides detailed insight into what is happening on the devices that are often the first targets in a cyberattack. EDR excels at identifying behavioral anomalies and suspicious patterns that may signify an active compromise. However, EDR's focus is inherently limited to what occurs on the endpoint itself. It lacks the visibility into network traffic, cloud environments, authentication systems, and third-party applications that are often critical to understanding the full scope of an attack.

SIEM platforms, by contrast, collect and normalize logs from a wide variety of sources, including firewalls, intrusion detection systems, cloud services, databases, application servers, and identity management systems. They offer a bird's-eye view of the entire environment and enable advanced correlation and rule-based analysis across disparate data points. This broad perspective is valuable for spotting multi-vector attacks, identifying patterns across time and systems, and supporting compliance and reporting requirements. However, SIEM systems may struggle to capture the granular detail and behavioral nuance available at the endpoint level, especially without a dedicated EDR feed.

By integrating EDR with a SIEM platform, organizations gain the ability to correlate detailed endpoint activity with broader network and system-level data. This union enhances threat detection by uncovering connections that may not be evident when each system operates in isolation. For example, a suspicious process detected by the EDR may be correlated with anomalous network behavior seen in firewall logs or with an unusual login pattern identified in Active Directory logs. Such multi-source correlation enables security teams to validate alerts, reduce false positives, and build a more complete picture of the threat. The enriched context also aids in prioritizing incidents, helping analysts focus on the most urgent and impactful threats.

Integration typically involves forwarding EDR telemetry and alerts to the SIEM in a standardized format, such as Syslog or through APIs and data connectors provided by the respective vendors. Once ingested, the SIEM can parse, index, and correlate the data with other log sources. Many SIEM solutions offer built-in support or specialized plugins for popular EDR platforms, streamlining the integration process and ensuring compatibility with existing analysis and visualization tools. Advanced configurations allow for bidirectional communication, where not only is EDR data sent to the SIEM, but the SIEM can also trigger response actions through the EDR based on correlated insights. This enables automated threat containment across systems and reduces the time between detection and response.

Another key advantage of EDR-SIEM integration is improved threat hunting capabilities. Analysts can use the SIEM's querying language to search across both endpoint and network data in a unified interface. This allows for complex investigations that might begin with an indicator on an endpoint and expand to encompass related activity across the enterprise. Threat hunting becomes more powerful when the analyst has access to both granular endpoint telemetry and high-level system logs, enabling the discovery of stealthy threats that evade conventional detection methods. The integration supports hypothesis-driven investigations and enables iterative analysis, where findings from one data source inform the next steps in the hunt.

Incident response workflows are also enhanced through integration. When an alert is generated, the SIEM can automatically compile relevant context from EDR data, asset inventories, user information, and historical logs. This comprehensive incident view allows responders to assess the severity and scope of the event quickly. In orchestrated environments, the SIEM may initiate predefined response actions such as isolating the affected endpoint, revoking user credentials, or blocking IP addresses through integrated firewalls. These coordinated responses reduce dwell time and limit the attacker's ability to escalate privileges or move laterally within the network. The centralization of alert management and response actions within the SIEM improves efficiency and ensures consistent application of incident handling procedures.

Compliance and auditing efforts also benefit significantly from the integration. Regulatory frameworks often require organizations to demonstrate that they can detect, investigate, and respond to security incidents in a timely and effective manner. The SIEM's centralized logging and reporting capabilities make it easier to document these activities. When integrated with EDR, the SIEM can provide evidence of endpoint-level activity, detection logic, and response actions taken, all in one place. This simplifies audits and enhances the organization's ability to meet regulatory obligations, whether for GDPR, HIPAA, PCI DSS, or other industry-specific standards.

Integration of EDR with SIEM platforms is not without challenges. Data volume is a primary concern, as EDR telemetry can generate vast amounts of information. Without proper filtering, normalization, and indexing, this influx can overwhelm the SIEM's storage and processing capacity. To address this, organizations must implement data management strategies that prioritize high-value telemetry, use event sampling when appropriate, and ensure that parsing rules are optimized for performance. Another challenge is ensuring data fidelity and consistency across platforms. Timestamp mismatches, missing fields, or incompatible formats can hinder correlation and analysis. Careful planning, testing, and validation are necessary to maintain data integrity and usability.

Security team coordination is also essential. The integration must be supported by shared operational procedures and a common understanding of alert taxonomy, severity ratings, and escalation protocols. Analysts working in the SIEM environment must be trained to interpret EDR data, and vice versa. Collaboration between EDR and SIEM teams enhances cross-functional understanding and ensures that insights from both systems are leveraged effectively. Over time, feedback from the integrated workflow can lead to improved detection rules, refined response playbooks, and greater alignment between tactical operations and strategic security goals.

As the cybersecurity landscape continues to evolve, the ability to operate across multiple layers of the environment becomes increasingly important. Integrating EDR with SIEM platforms empowers organizations with both depth and breadth of visibility, enabling them to detect, investigate, and respond to threats with speed and precision. This integration represents the convergence of endpoint-level intelligence with enterprise-wide awareness, providing the foundation for intelligent, automated, and adaptive security operations capable of meeting the demands of the modern threat environment.

Incident Triage and Root Cause Analysis

In the rapidly shifting landscape of cybersecurity, one of the most critical capabilities for any security operations team is the ability to triage incidents effectively and conduct thorough root cause analysis. These two processes are central to the efficient handling of security events detected by Endpoint Detection and Response systems. Triage allows security teams to quickly assess the urgency and impact of an alert, while root cause analysis enables them to understand how and why the incident occurred. Together, they form the core of an intelligent, responsive, and continuously improving security posture. Without effective triage, organizations are left overwhelmed by alert volumes, and without accurate root cause analysis, they risk repeated compromises from unresolved vulnerabilities.

Incident triage begins the moment a security alert is generated. Modern EDR platforms constantly monitor endpoint behavior for signs of malicious activity, generating alerts when they detect anomalies or indicators of compromise. However, not all alerts are equal. Some represent genuine threats requiring immediate action, while others may be false positives or low-risk events that do not demand urgent attention. Triage is the process of sorting these alerts based on their severity, potential impact, and likelihood of being malicious. This step is essential to ensure that limited security resources are focused on the incidents that pose the greatest risk to the organization.

Effective triage involves evaluating multiple dimensions of the alert. These include the confidence level assigned by the detection engine, the nature of the behavior observed, the identity of the user or system involved, and any associated threat intelligence. For example, an alert involving the execution of PowerShell with obfuscated arguments by a non-administrative user may warrant immediate attention, especially if it coincides with outbound network connections to known malicious domains. In contrast, an alert triggered by an unusual but explainable file access by a trusted administrator might be deprioritized or closed after a brief review. This decision-making process must be both fast and accurate, requiring tools that present relevant context and visualizations to help analysts make informed judgments.

Automated triage mechanisms can greatly enhance the efficiency of this process. EDR platforms often incorporate scoring systems that prioritize alerts based on dynamic risk assessments. These systems consider behavioral indicators, asset sensitivity, historical patterns, and correlations with other data sources. Alerts with high-risk scores are automatically escalated for analyst review, while low-confidence alerts may be suppressed or routed for deferred analysis. Automation does not eliminate the need for human judgment, but it does reduce the volume of alerts that must be manually assessed, allowing security analysts to focus their efforts where they matter most.

Once an alert is triaged and determined to represent a real threat, the next step is to conduct root cause analysis. This is the process of identifying the origin and full context of the incident, including how the attacker gained access, what tactics were used, and what vulnerabilities or weaknesses were exploited. Root cause analysis is critical for understanding the scope of the incident, containing its effects, and preventing recurrence. Without this deeper understanding, security teams are left treating symptoms rather than addressing the underlying issues that enabled the attack.

Root cause analysis begins with timeline reconstruction. EDR tools provide detailed telemetry from the affected endpoint, including process execution trees, file access logs, registry changes, and network activity. Analysts use this information to build a sequence of events that shows how the attack unfolded. For example, the analysis might reveal that a malicious document was opened by a user, which then triggered a macro that launched a hidden script. The script may have created a scheduled task to maintain persistence, connected to a command and control server, and downloaded additional payloads. Each of these steps must be identified and examined to understand the attacker's objectives and techniques.

In addition to identifying what happened, root cause analysis must determine why it happened. This involves identifying the initial entry point and the vulnerabilities that were exploited. Common entry points include phishing emails, exposed remote desktop services, weak credentials, and unpatched software. Analysts must trace the attack back to its earliest observable action and determine whether it was preventable. This often requires reviewing security controls, user behavior, and patch management practices. The goal is to identify gaps in the organization's defenses that allowed the attacker to succeed. These findings inform the development of corrective actions and long-term improvements to the organization's security posture.

Collaboration is a key element in effective root cause analysis. Analysts must often coordinate with IT operations, system administrators, application owners, and sometimes third-party vendors to gather additional information and validate findings. For example, understanding whether a configuration change was intentional or unauthorized may require input from the system owner. Root cause analysis is not just a technical task but an investigative effort that spans multiple roles and departments. Clear communication, detailed documentation, and strong organizational processes are essential for ensuring that the analysis is accurate, complete, and actionable.

The outcome of root cause analysis should be a clear report that details the incident timeline, root cause, scope of impact, and recommended remediation actions. This report serves as the foundation for both immediate response efforts and longer-term security improvements. It should include specific technical findings, such as indicators of compromise and exploited vulnerabilities, as well as strategic recommendations, such as policy changes, security awareness training, or technology upgrades. The report may also be used for compliance reporting, post-incident reviews, and executive briefings, making clarity and accuracy essential.

Over time, the insights gained through incident triage and root cause analysis contribute to the organization's collective threat intelligence and institutional knowledge. Patterns begin to emerge, allowing security teams to identify common attack vectors, recurring vulnerabilities, and systemic weaknesses. This feedback loop enables continuous improvement in detection rules, response playbooks, and security architecture. For example, if multiple incidents trace back to credential phishing, the organization may decide to implement multi-factor authentication and enhance email filtering capabilities. If certain types of behavior are consistently misclassified, detection logic can be refined to improve accuracy.

Incident triage and root cause analysis are essential processes in transforming security operations from reactive to proactive. Triage ensures that the most dangerous threats receive immediate attention, while root cause analysis provides the understanding necessary to prevent future incidents. Together, they enable organizations to respond swiftly, learn continuously, and build resilience against a constantly evolving threat landscape. These processes are not merely technical tasks but strategic functions that align with the organization's overall risk management goals. By investing in the people, processes, and technologies that support effective triage and root cause analysis, organizations position themselves to withstand the challenges of modern cyber threats with confidence and clarity.

Threat Intelligence in EDR

The integration of threat intelligence into Endpoint Detection and Response systems represents a major advancement in the ability of security teams to detect, understand, and neutralize threats with speed and precision. Threat intelligence refers to the curated knowledge about adversaries, including their tools, tactics, techniques, procedures, infrastructure, and behavioral patterns. This information can be gathered from external sources, internal telemetry, or a combination of both. When properly integrated into EDR, threat intelligence transforms raw endpoint data into actionable insights, enabling a proactive security stance and empowering organizations to stay ahead of emerging threats.

At the core of any EDR platform is the ability to monitor, analyze, and respond to activity on endpoints. While these platforms are highly effective in detecting abnormal behavior, they become significantly more powerful when their detection logic is informed by up-to-date threat intelligence. This intelligence adds context to the activities observed on endpoints, allowing the system to make more accurate assessments of risk. For instance, a process communicating with an IP address may not appear malicious on its own, but if that IP is known to be associated with a command and control server used by a specific malware family, the detection becomes much more meaningful. The correlation between endpoint telemetry and external threat indicators enables faster identification of known threats and increases the confidence of alerts.

Threat intelligence comes in many forms and can be categorized into strategic, operational, tactical, and technical levels. Strategic intelligence provides high-level insights into threat actors, including their motivations and objectives. Operational intelligence includes details about attack campaigns, while tactical intelligence focuses on the tools and techniques used in attacks. Technical intelligence is the most granular and consists of indicators of compromise such as IP addresses, domain names, file hashes, and email addresses. EDR systems primarily rely on technical and tactical intelligence, using this information to match observed endpoint behaviors with known malicious patterns.

The integration process typically involves feeding threat intelligence into the EDR platform through APIs, file uploads, or subscriptions to threat intelligence feeds. These feeds may be provided by commercial vendors, open-source communities, government agencies, or industry-specific information sharing and analysis centers. Once ingested, the EDR system uses the intelligence to enrich alerts, flag suspicious behavior, and support automated responses. For example, if a newly discovered malware hash is added to the threat feed, the EDR system can immediately scan all endpoints to determine if that file is present, quarantine affected devices, and notify analysts of the findings. This rapid dissemination of intelligence allows for a near-instantaneous response to global threats.

One of the most valuable uses of threat intelligence in EDR is the detection of previously undetected threats. Security teams may use intelligence to retroactively analyze historical data, uncovering signs of compromise that were not flagged at the time of occurrence. This process, known as threat hunting, allows analysts to pivot from threat intelligence indicators and trace their presence across endpoint data. By identifying patterns that align with known threat actor behavior, analysts can uncover hidden campaigns and determine whether adversaries have already established a foothold in the environment. This proactive approach is especially effective against advanced persistent threats that operate with stealth and persistence over extended periods.

Threat intelligence also enhances the effectiveness of automated response actions. When the EDR platform is aware that a particular domain is associated with a phishing campaign or that a specific process is used by ransomware, it can initiate predefined playbooks to isolate the endpoint, terminate the process, or block outbound traffic. This immediate response capability shortens the window of exposure and limits the attacker's ability to execute their objectives.

Furthermore, when threat intelligence is shared across integrated systems such as SIEMs, firewalls, and cloud platforms, the entire security ecosystem becomes more coordinated and resilient.

Contextual enrichment is another benefit of integrating threat intelligence with EDR. Alerts generated by the system are often accompanied by metadata such as confidence scores, threat actor attribution, attack severity, and recommended remediation steps. This information helps analysts triage incidents more effectively and make faster decisions about how to respond. Instead of spending valuable time researching an alert, the analyst has immediate access to contextual data that supports decision-making. This efficiency improves incident response times and enhances the overall effectiveness of the security team.

Organizations can also generate their own internal threat intelligence by analyzing incidents that occur within their environment. This intelligence, often referred to as closed-loop or internal threat intelligence, can include custom indicators, behavior patterns observed in targeted attacks, and unique artifacts specific to the organization's infrastructure. When fed back into the EDR system, this intelligence helps to strengthen detection capabilities against threats that may not yet be widely known or reported externally. Internal intelligence is particularly valuable for identifying insider threats, supply chain compromises, and attacks that exploit organization-specific configurations.

The value of threat intelligence in EDR increases over time as the system continuously ingests new data, learns from incidents, and refines its detection logic. Machine learning models can be trained on threat intelligence data to recognize emerging attack patterns and predict future threats. These predictive capabilities extend the reach of the EDR system beyond known indicators and into the realm of adaptive security. By understanding how threat actors evolve their tactics, the system becomes better equipped to anticipate their moves and prevent successful compromises.

To fully realize the benefits of threat intelligence, organizations must ensure that their intelligence sources are reliable, relevant, and timely. Not all threat feeds are equal, and ingesting low-quality or outdated indicators can introduce noise and increase the risk of false positives. Security teams must evaluate threat intelligence providers based on the accuracy, context, and frequency of their updates. In many cases, blending multiple sources of intelligence, including commercial and open-source feeds, provides the most comprehensive and balanced view of the threat landscape.

Finally, the success of threat intelligence in EDR depends on the people who use it. Analysts must be trained to interpret and apply intelligence data effectively, understanding the relationships between indicators, behaviors, and threat actors. Collaboration between threat intelligence teams and endpoint response teams is essential to ensure that intelligence is not only consumed but also acted upon. Continuous feedback between these groups improves the relevance and impact of the intelligence, making it an integral part of the organization's security lifecycle.

Threat intelligence is not simply about collecting data; it is about enhancing situational awareness, informing decisions, and enabling faster, more accurate responses. In the context of EDR, it provides the lens through which raw telemetry is transformed into actionable knowledge. As cyber threats continue to evolve in speed, scale, and sophistication, the integration of threat intelligence into endpoint security operations becomes not just advantageous but indispensable for organizations committed to robust, intelligent defense.

Forensic Capabilities of Modern EDR Tools

Modern Endpoint Detection and Response tools have significantly expanded the role of digital forensics in cybersecurity by bringing forensic capabilities directly to the endpoint level in real time. These tools are no longer limited to reactive investigation after a breach has occurred. Instead, they provide continuous monitoring, logging, and data retention features that enable immediate visibility into suspicious behaviors, detailed reconstruction of attack paths, and rapid access to historical data. The forensic capabilities built into modern EDR platforms empower security analysts to act faster, investigate deeper, and respond more intelligently to complex cyber threats. By integrating these features into day-to-day security operations, EDR tools have redefined the standards of incident response and digital evidence collection.

One of the core elements of forensic capability within EDR systems is their ability to maintain a continuous and detailed record of endpoint activity. Unlike traditional forensic tools that require physical access to a device and manual imaging of drives, EDR agents collect telemetry in real time and transmit it to a centralized system where it can be stored, indexed, and queried. This telemetry includes data on process execution, file modifications, registry access, user logins, command-line arguments, network connections, and inter-process communications. With this level of granularity, analysts can perform forensic investigations without needing to physically interact with the compromised device, dramatically reducing the time and logistical complexity involved in incident response.

Process lineage tracking is one of the most powerful forensic features provided by EDR platforms. By capturing the parent-child relationships between processes and preserving the full execution chain, analysts can trace the origin of a malicious process back to its point of initiation. This is critical for understanding how a threat entered the system, whether it was delivered via phishing, dropped by another payload, or initiated through a vulnerable application. Knowing the process lineage helps determine whether the execution was automated, user-initiated, or part of a script, which can inform decisions about remediation and prevention. In some cases, analysts can follow the execution trail back several steps to discover the initial infection vector and any lateral movement that may have occurred.

Another valuable forensic function is memory analysis. Many modern attacks, especially those involving fileless malware, operate entirely within system memory, leaving no artifacts on disk for traditional tools to capture. EDR tools that incorporate memory scanning and process introspection can identify in-memory injection techniques, shellcode execution, and the presence of anomalous memory segments that suggest a running threat. These insights are invaluable for detecting advanced threats that rely on evasion and stealth. In volatile memory, attackers may store payloads, maintain command-and-control sessions, or execute credential theft operations. By analyzing this data in real time, EDR solutions can detect these tactics as they occur and preserve the forensic artifacts necessary for full investigation.

File access auditing is another cornerstone of EDR forensic capabilities. These tools monitor every file operation on the endpoint, including creation, deletion, read, write, and permission changes. Each action is logged with precise metadata, such as the user involved, timestamp, associated process, and hash of the file before and after modification. This level of auditing enables investigators to determine what data was targeted, whether it was exfiltrated, and whether any sensitive or regulated information was accessed during an attack. In cases involving ransomware, file access logs can help determine the extent of encryption and identify which files can be recovered from backups or volume shadow copies.

User activity monitoring adds another layer to forensic investigation by correlating endpoint behavior with human interaction. EDR systems record login attempts, session durations, privilege escalations, and authentication anomalies. By tying these events to process and file activity, investigators can distinguish between legitimate administrative actions and those performed by compromised accounts or insider threats. This is especially important in environments where attackers use stolen credentials to mask their activities. Forensic analysis of user behavior helps establish intent, identify the insider risk, and support legal or disciplinary proceedings when necessary.

Network activity visibility is also critical for endpoint-level forensics. EDR platforms monitor outbound and inbound connections from each endpoint, capturing data such as destination IP addresses, ports, protocols, and domain names. This information can be used to identify exfiltration channels, lateral movement attempts, or communications with known command-and-control infrastructure. The ability to match these connections with threat intelligence feeds and historical data provides context that enhances the accuracy and depth of investigations. Additionally, EDR tools may log DNS queries and responses, enabling analysts to uncover domain generation algorithms or fast flux networks commonly used in evasive campaigns.

The capability to conduct retrospective analysis is one of the major advantages that forensic features in EDR systems provide. Since telemetry data is stored over an extended period, analysts can go back in time to review endpoint activity from weeks or months before a threat was discovered. This allows for detection of slow-moving attacks that unfold over long durations, as well as the identification of patient zero in a widespread infection. Retrospective analysis also supports legal and compliance requirements by providing a reliable, time-stamped audit trail that demonstrates how incidents were handled and what data may have been impacted.

EDR systems enhance evidence preservation by automatically collecting and storing critical data when suspicious activity is detected. This ensures that forensic artifacts are not lost due to normal system activity, data retention policies, or intentional tampering by attackers. Some platforms include snapshot capabilities that can capture the system state at the time of detection, including memory, open handles, running threads, and system configurations. These snapshots can be invaluable for recreating the environment as it existed during the attack, providing a complete view for investigators or third-party examiners.

Modern EDR tools also support remote forensics, which is particularly important in distributed or hybrid work environments. Analysts can investigate endpoints regardless of geographic location, pull forensic data on demand, and execute targeted commands to gather additional evidence. This remote access reduces the delay in responding to incidents and allows for timely containment and investigation without waiting for physical access. Remote forensic capabilities enable organizations to maintain control over security operations even in decentralized workforces, where endpoints may connect from untrusted networks or personal devices.

Finally, the forensic capabilities of EDR systems contribute to long-term security improvements. By understanding how an attacker succeeded, what tools were used, and where defenses failed, organizations can implement targeted controls to prevent recurrence. This may include patching vulnerabilities, updating detection logic, enhancing user training, or improving access controls. Forensic findings also inform red teaming exercises, incident simulations, and threat modeling activities that raise overall security maturity. The depth and speed of forensic analysis provided by EDR platforms allow organizations to turn every incident into an opportunity for learning and resilience.

The forensic capabilities embedded in modern EDR tools have fundamentally changed how organizations approach incident response and investigation. No longer restricted to post-incident evidence gathering, forensic analysis can now occur in real time, at scale, and with far greater precision than ever before. This evolution allows security teams to not only react to threats more effectively but also understand them at a forensic level, enabling informed decisions, rapid containment, and robust prevention strategies that strengthen the organization's entire security framework.

Cloud-Based EDR Architectures

The evolution of Endpoint Detection and Response solutions into cloud-based architectures marks a significant advancement in cybersecurity, addressing the limitations of traditional on-premises systems and adapting to the demands of modern, distributed enterprise environments. As organizations increasingly adopt cloud services, hybrid infrastructures, and remote work models, the need for scalable, agile, and globally accessible security solutions has grown in parallel. Cloud-based EDR architectures have emerged in response to this shift, offering enhanced visibility, real-time threat detection, rapid deployment, and centralized management across geographically dispersed endpoints. These platforms leverage the power of cloud computing to deliver more effective and efficient protection, while also addressing operational and scalability challenges that were difficult or impossible to overcome with traditional models.

A cloud-based EDR system typically consists of lightweight endpoint agents installed on devices, connected to a centralized cloud platform that processes, analyzes, and stores telemetry data. The agents continuously monitor endpoint behavior, capturing data on process execution, network activity, file changes, and system events. This data is then streamed to the cloud where it is aggregated and analyzed using advanced algorithms, behavioral models, and threat intelligence feeds. By shifting the heavy processing load to the cloud, endpoint agents can remain lightweight and unobtrusive, minimizing impact on device performance while still providing deep visibility into endpoint activity.

One of the most compelling advantages of cloud-based EDR architectures is their ability to scale dynamically with organizational growth. Traditional EDR systems often require significant investment in infrastructure, including servers, storage, and network bandwidth, to support large numbers of endpoints. Managing and maintaining this infrastructure presents logistical and financial burdens, especially for organizations with limited IT resources. In contrast, cloud-based EDR platforms scale elastically, allowing organizations to onboard thousands of endpoints without worrying about hardware limitations or infrastructure upgrades. The elasticity of cloud environments ensures that performance remains consistent, regardless of the number of endpoints being monitored or the volume of telemetry being processed.

Cloud-based EDR solutions also offer superior speed and agility in both deployment and operations. Agents can be deployed remotely across all devices in the enterprise, including those outside the corporate network or in remote locations. This remote deployability is crucial in modern work environments where employees operate from home, satellite offices, or while traveling. Cloud connectivity ensures that even off-network devices maintain full security coverage and continue to send telemetry to the central platform. Updates to detection rules, threat intelligence, and response playbooks can be pushed out instantly from the cloud to all endpoints, eliminating the delays associated with manual patching and rule updates in traditional systems.

Centralized management is another powerful feature of cloud-based EDR platforms. Security teams can monitor, investigate, and respond to threats from a single console, regardless of the physical location of the endpoints. This centralized approach reduces complexity and enhances operational efficiency by providing consistent visibility and control across the entire enterprise. Analysts can access real-time dashboards, perform threat hunts, investigate alerts, and initiate response actions without needing to connect to multiple systems or navigate fragmented data sources. This unified view of security events accelerates detection and response, ensuring that threats are addressed before they can escalate into full-blown incidents.

Data analytics is a core strength of cloud-based architectures. The massive computational power available in the cloud allows for real-time analysis of vast amounts of endpoint telemetry. Machine learning and artificial intelligence algorithms are employed to identify patterns, detect anomalies, and uncover subtle indicators of compromise that might be missed by signature-based approaches. These models are continuously trained on global threat data and updated automatically in the cloud, allowing the system to stay ahead of emerging threats without requiring manual intervention. The combination of cloud scale and intelligent analytics significantly enhances the accuracy, speed, and depth of threat detection.

Cloud-based EDR systems also facilitate better collaboration between security teams, especially in organizations with distributed or global operations. Multiple analysts can work simultaneously within the platform, sharing investigation notes, assigning tasks, and collaborating on incident response workflows. Integrated case management tools and automated playbooks streamline coordination and ensure that incidents are handled consistently and efficiently. In high-pressure situations, such as responding to a ransomware outbreak, this collaborative capability is invaluable in maintaining order and accelerating containment efforts.

Security and compliance are frequently cited concerns when moving critical security functions to the cloud, but modern cloud-based EDR platforms address these challenges through robust encryption, access controls, and regulatory compliance features. Telemetry data is encrypted in transit and at rest, and strict authentication protocols ensure that only authorized personnel can access sensitive information. Many cloud EDR providers undergo regular third-party audits and offer compliance certifications for standards such as GDPR, HIPAA, ISO 27001, and SOC 2. Organizations can also configure data retention policies and geographic storage locations to align with legal and regulatory requirements, further enhancing trust in cloud-based operations.

Cloud-native EDR platforms offer significant advantages for threat hunting and forensic investigation. The centralized storage of historical telemetry data enables long-term analysis of endpoint behavior, helping analysts identify patterns of compromise that develop over extended periods. Threat hunters can query this data using advanced search tools and filters, pivot between related events, and build timelines that reveal the full scope of an attack. This retrospective analysis capability allows teams to uncover dormant threats, identify patient zero, and validate whether attackers have been fully eradicated from the environment. Forensic data that once required manual collection and analysis can now be accessed instantly and remotely through a single interface.

The integration potential of cloud-based EDR systems with other security tools enhances the overall security ecosystem. These platforms often offer APIs and prebuilt connectors for SIEMs, SOAR platforms, threat intelligence feeds, identity providers, and vulnerability management systems. This interoperability ensures that EDR data is shared across tools, enriching alerts, supporting correlation rules, and enabling orchestrated response actions. For example, a threat detected by the EDR can automatically trigger a firewall rule update, a user account lockout, or a notification in a team collaboration channel, all within seconds. The result is a more cohesive and responsive security posture that adapts to the speed and complexity of modern threats.

As organizations continue to adopt hybrid and cloud-first strategies, cloud-based EDR architectures are becoming the default choice for endpoint security. They align with the demands of flexibility, scalability, and continuous protection, delivering high-performance detection and response capabilities that are not bound by physical infrastructure. By leveraging the power of the cloud, these systems empower security teams to operate with greater agility, insight, and resilience, ensuring that they can meet the evolving challenges of the threat landscape with confidence and control.

Endpoint Isolation Techniques

Endpoint isolation is a critical containment strategy in modern cybersecurity, particularly within the context of Endpoint Detection and Response platforms. As attackers become more sophisticated and faster in their methods, organizations must be prepared to respond with equal speed to prevent lateral movement, data exfiltration, and system compromise. Isolation provides a way to swiftly contain threats by limiting or severing the endpoint's communication with other systems or the internet without completely disabling the device. This approach allows for continued investigation, remediation, and even user interaction when necessary, all while minimizing the risk of further spread or impact. Effective endpoint isolation techniques are essential to the success of incident response efforts and the overall resilience of enterprise environments.

The concept of isolation begins with identifying a potentially compromised endpoint through real-time detection or alert triage. Once a device is flagged as suspicious or confirmed to be part of an active threat, isolation can be triggered either automatically by the EDR platform or manually by a security analyst. The isolation process involves a set of technical actions that restrict the endpoint's ability to communicate with its surroundings, thereby containing any malicious activity that might be in progress. This step is taken with the primary goal of preventing the threat from propagating to other systems while preserving the current state of the device for forensic analysis and further inspection.

Network-level isolation is the most commonly used technique and one of the most effective. It involves blocking all inbound and outbound traffic from the endpoint, except for the communication needed to maintain the connection between the device and the EDR platform. This ensures that the endpoint can still report telemetry and receive response commands from the central console, but it is otherwise cut off from the internal network and the broader internet. This method is highly effective in halting command and control communication, stopping data exfiltration attempts, and preventing malware from spreading. Because the EDR agent remains active, analysts can continue monitoring the device, pulling forensic data, and executing response actions even while it is isolated.

Another form of isolation is process-level containment, which focuses on restricting or terminating specific processes that have been identified as malicious or suspicious. This method is particularly useful when the entire endpoint does not need to be cut off from the network but where one or more processes are engaging in harmful behavior. By terminating these processes or placing them in a sandboxed state, the threat is neutralized without disrupting the user's legitimate work or other system operations. Some EDR platforms go a step further by suspending process execution until further analysis is performed, allowing analysts to make informed decisions before allowing the process to continue.

In more advanced isolation strategies, file-level controls are employed. This includes quarantining specific files or scripts that are suspected of being malicious. Quarantine involves moving the file to a secure, isolated location on the endpoint where it cannot be executed, modified, or accessed by other processes. This prevents the file from being part of an active attack while retaining it for later analysis. Quarantined files can be hashed, scanned with additional engines, or submitted to sandbox environments for dynamic analysis. File isolation can be particularly helpful in managing malware samples, suspicious installers, or scripts found in email attachments or download directories.

Virtual network segmentation is also used to isolate endpoints by dynamically placing them into isolated virtual LANs or VLANs. This technique allows the endpoint to remain operational but limits its ability to communicate with critical systems or sensitive segments of the network. Dynamic segmentation is especially useful in organizations with software-defined networking capabilities, as it allows for flexible, policy-driven isolation that adapts to the context of the incident. Devices can be moved into quarantine zones based on the severity of the alert or the classification of the threat, offering a layered approach to containment that minimizes disruption while maximizing security.

Behavioral-based isolation is an emerging technique that leverages machine learning and analytics to determine when an endpoint's behavior deviates significantly from its established baseline. Instead of relying solely on signatures or known indicators of compromise, the system flags and isolates endpoints that show unusual activity patterns, such as abnormal file access rates, unexpected privilege escalations, or unauthorized command execution. Behavioral isolation allows for faster containment of unknown or zero-day threats that may not yet have clear indicators. Once isolated, these endpoints can be analyzed in detail to determine whether the behavior was benign or malicious, and the system can adjust its models accordingly.

Isolation techniques are often combined with endpoint deception technologies that confuse or mislead attackers. When a threat is detected, the endpoint can be isolated and redirected to interact with decoy systems or files that simulate a production environment. These decoys serve to waste the attacker's time, gather intelligence about their tactics, and protect real assets from harm. Deception-based isolation adds an active defense layer that not only contains but also counteracts threats in a controlled and monitored way.

The effectiveness of endpoint isolation depends not only on the technical mechanisms used but also on the speed and accuracy of execution. Timely isolation can prevent an attack from becoming a full-scale breach. Many EDR platforms support automated isolation based on preconfigured policies and detection rules, ensuring that endpoints are isolated immediately upon detection of high-risk behaviors. However, manual isolation is often used when analysts require discretion or when alerts are less certain. Regardless of the trigger method, the ability to isolate endpoints within seconds of identifying a threat is a key factor in minimizing damage.

Isolation must also be reversible and manageable. Once the investigation concludes and remediation is complete, the endpoint should be restored to full connectivity in a controlled and secure manner. EDR platforms provide mechanisms to remove isolation, confirm that the threat has been neutralized, and document the actions taken. This includes verifying that the system is clean, updating configurations or software, and possibly re-imaging the device. A successful isolation and recovery cycle not only prevents ongoing damage but also reinforces organizational confidence in the incident response process.

Training and preparedness are essential to effective endpoint isolation. Security teams must be familiar with the tools and procedures involved in isolating endpoints and know how to communicate clearly with affected users. Isolation can be disruptive, especially if critical systems or high-value users are involved. Clear policies and communication protocols help ensure that isolation is seen as a protective measure rather than a punitive or arbitrary action. User awareness and support are important components of maintaining cooperation and reducing resistance during incident response.

Endpoint isolation techniques have become indispensable tools in the cybersecurity arsenal. They provide immediate containment, support forensic investigation, and enable coordinated response efforts without requiring physical access or full shutdown of devices. As threats continue to increase in complexity and speed, isolation remains one of the most effective ways to halt attacks in their tracks and protect the broader environment from compromise. Through a combination of network, process, file, and behavioral controls, modern EDR platforms offer flexible and powerful isolation capabilities that are essential for rapid, intelligent, and effective threat response.

Containment Strategies and Limitations

Containment is a fundamental objective of incident response and a core capability of Endpoint Detection and Response platforms. It refers to the set of actions taken to limit the scope and impact of a security incident once a threat has been detected. The primary goal is to prevent the attacker from achieving their objectives, whether those include data exfiltration, lateral movement, privilege escalation, or persistence. By effectively containing a threat, organizations can reduce the damage inflicted, maintain business continuity, and create the conditions necessary for thorough investigation and recovery. While containment is critical to limiting the reach of cyberattacks, it is not without its limitations. The effectiveness of containment depends on timing, precision, technology capabilities, and the sophistication of the adversary.

Containment strategies are generally categorized into immediate and strategic containment. Immediate containment is executed as soon as a threat is detected, focusing on stopping the attacker's current actions. This may involve isolating an endpoint, terminating malicious processes, blocking network connections, disabling user accounts, or restricting access to sensitive systems. These actions are intended to halt the threat as quickly as possible before it spreads or causes additional harm. Immediate containment is typically driven by automated response mechanisms or predefined playbooks that allow security teams to act without delay. In some cases, manual intervention is necessary, particularly when the context of the alert is unclear or when business-critical systems are involved.

Strategic containment involves longer-term actions aimed at addressing the broader context of the attack. This can include reconfiguring firewalls, segmenting the network, patching vulnerabilities, updating policies, or conducting user awareness training. Strategic containment looks beyond the immediate symptoms to address the underlying conditions that allowed the incident to occur. It plays a crucial role in preventing recurrence and strengthening the overall security posture. While strategic containment takes more time to implement, it complements immediate containment by offering more durable solutions to systemic issues.

One of the most widely used containment techniques in EDR platforms is endpoint isolation. This action prevents the affected device from communicating with other systems, thereby cutting off the attacker's access to the network. Isolation is highly effective in halting data exfiltration and lateral movement, and it preserves the state of the device for forensic investigation. However, isolation is not without limitations. It may disrupt legitimate business operations, especially if the endpoint belongs to a critical user or system. Furthermore, if the attacker has already moved laterally or established persistence elsewhere, isolating one endpoint may not be enough to contain the full threat.

Another common containment tactic is process termination. When a process is identified as malicious, the EDR system can force it to stop, preventing it from continuing its execution. This action is particularly useful against ransomware, keyloggers, and data stealers. Terminating a process can quickly neutralize the immediate threat, but it does not guarantee that the threat actor is eliminated from the environment. In some cases, attackers may deploy multiple payloads or use scheduled tasks, registry keys, or alternate binaries to reinitiate their activities. Without addressing the root cause and the full extent of the compromise, process termination alone may be insufficient.

Network containment measures include blocking specific IP addresses, domains, or ports associated with the threat. EDR platforms often integrate with firewalls or network access control systems to facilitate such actions. Network containment is effective in stopping command-and-control traffic and preventing malware from downloading additional components. However, advanced attackers may use fast-flux DNS, encrypted communications, or legitimate cloud services to bypass these controls. In such cases, static blocklists may not provide adequate protection, and more dynamic analysis or behavioral monitoring may be required.

User account containment is also a vital strategy, particularly when dealing with credential theft or insider threats. Disabling or locking compromised accounts can prevent attackers from leveraging stolen credentials to escalate privileges or access additional systems. This strategy is especially relevant in environments where identity-based attacks are common. The challenge lies in distinguishing between legitimate and malicious use of credentials, particularly in the case of privilege misuse or shared accounts. Locking out a legitimate user during a critical operation can have significant business repercussions, so containment actions must be based on high-confidence detections.

Containment strategies must be supported by clear policies and well-rehearsed procedures. Without predefined guidelines, security teams may hesitate to act, leading to delays that allow threats to escalate. Response playbooks that define containment actions for specific scenarios, such as ransomware outbreaks or phishing campaigns, provide clarity and consistency in high-pressure situations. These playbooks should be reviewed and updated regularly to reflect new threats and changes in the IT environment. They should also include escalation paths and decision-making criteria to guide analysts when full automation is not appropriate.

The limitations of containment are often related to detection accuracy and timing. If a threat is not detected early enough, containment measures may be applied too late to prevent significant damage. Similarly, false positives can lead to unnecessary containment actions that disrupt business operations and erode trust in the security system. Achieving the right balance between aggressive containment and operational continuity requires accurate threat detection, context-aware analysis, and risk-based decision-making. Overreliance on automated containment without adequate oversight can lead to unintended consequences, while overly cautious approaches may fail to stop threats in time.

Resource constraints can also limit containment effectiveness. In large environments with thousands of endpoints, simultaneous containment actions can strain network infrastructure and management systems. Additionally, organizations with small or understaffed security teams may struggle to investigate and contain multiple incidents at once. Automation helps mitigate these limitations, but it must be implemented thoughtfully to ensure scalability, resilience, and alignment with organizational priorities.

Containment must also consider the possibility of adversarial adaptation. Sophisticated attackers are aware of standard containment techniques and may build resilience into their operations. They might use redundant command-and-control channels, deploy fallback payloads, or monitor for isolation events to change tactics in real time. Some malware is programmed to self-destruct or delete logs when containment is detected, complicating forensic analysis. To counter these tactics, containment strategies should include deception, monitoring, and fail-safe mechanisms that continue to gather intelligence and maintain visibility even during an active response.

Communication is another critical component of effective containment. Internal stakeholders, including IT, legal, HR, and executive leadership, must be informed about containment actions and their potential impact. Clear communication helps manage expectations, coordinate remediation, and maintain transparency during a security incident. In regulated industries, external reporting may also be required, making accurate and timely communication even more important. Containment strategies should include communication protocols that ensure the right information reaches the right people at the right time.

While containment is an indispensable component of incident response, it is not a solution in itself. It must be integrated into a broader lifecycle that includes detection, analysis, eradication, recovery, and post-incident review. The limitations of containment underscore the need for continuous improvement, proactive defense, and a layered security architecture. When combined with strategic planning, robust detection, and comprehensive remediation, containment becomes a powerful tool for defending against modern threats and protecting the integrity of enterprise systems.

User and Entity Behavior Analytics

User and Entity Behavior Analytics, often abbreviated as UEBA, is a sophisticated approach to threat detection that has become increasingly vital in the realm of Endpoint Detection and Response. As attackers grow more adept at blending into legitimate activity and evading traditional security controls, security teams need tools that go beyond static indicators of compromise. UEBA fills this gap by focusing on what users and systems normally do and identifying deviations from these behavioral baselines that could signal malicious intent or compromise. This shift from signature-based detection to behavior-based analysis enables a deeper, more contextual understanding of threats and enhances the organization's ability to detect insider threats, compromised accounts, and stealthy intrusions.

At the core of UEBA is the concept of baseline behavior. Every user, device, application, and system within an organization exhibits patterns that, over time, form a predictable norm. These patterns include login times, resource access, network usage, file interactions, and application behavior. UEBA systems collect and analyze these patterns to establish what is typical for each entity. Once the baselines are in place, the system continuously monitors for anomalies—actions that deviate significantly from the established norms. These anomalies may indicate suspicious activity such as an employee accessing files they have never used before, a user logging in from a foreign country at an unusual time, or a service account performing administrative functions it was not designed for.

UEBA systems use advanced statistical models, machine learning algorithms, and contextual data to differentiate between benign anomalies and genuinely suspicious behavior. Not all deviations are malicious. For example, a user logging in from a different city may be traveling, or a burst of activity might be explained by a temporary project. Machine learning helps UEBA systems to reduce false positives by learning from feedback and continuously adapting to the evolving behavior of users and systems. Over time, these systems become more effective at distinguishing noise from real threats, providing security teams with high-confidence alerts that merit investigation.

One of the most significant advantages of UEBA is its ability to detect insider threats. Traditional security systems are often focused on external threats, using firewalls, antivirus software, and intrusion detection systems to block unauthorized access. However, threats from within—whether intentional or accidental—can be far more difficult to identify. Employees, contractors, and partners already have access to internal systems and data, which means their actions may not trigger conventional alarms. UEBA identifies when a legitimate user begins to behave in ways that are inconsistent with their historical profile. For instance, if a finance employee starts downloading large volumes of HR data or accessing engineering repositories at night, UEBA can flag these behaviors as potential indicators of data theft or account compromise.

Another important use case for UEBA is detecting account takeovers. Attackers often steal credentials through phishing, credential stuffing, or brute force attacks. Once inside the network, they may try to move laterally, escalate privileges, or access sensitive data. Because they are using valid credentials, many traditional detection systems may not flag their activity. UEBA can detect these intrusions by noticing that the account is being used in ways that differ from its historical norms. An engineer logging in from an unusual location and accessing databases never touched before is suspicious, even if they successfully authenticate. These subtle behavioral clues are key to catching attackers who are trying to hide in plain sight.

In the context of EDR, UEBA significantly enhances the ability to investigate and respond to endpoint-related incidents. By linking endpoint telemetry with user behavior, analysts gain a richer, more contextual view of security events. For example, when a suspicious process is launched on an endpoint, UEBA can help determine whether it was initiated by a user and whether that user's behavior has also changed in meaningful ways. This correlation provides important insights into the intent and scope of the activity, allowing security teams to prioritize and respond more effectively. It also supports root cause analysis by identifying whether the incident stemmed from a malicious actor, a misconfigured system, or a careless user.

UEBA also plays a key role in threat hunting, allowing analysts to proactively search for patterns of anomalous behavior across the environment. Rather than relying solely on alerts, threat hunters can query behavior models to identify users or entities that show signs of compromise or policy violation. These investigations might uncover slow-moving threats that evade traditional detection methods or reveal early warning signs of more complex attacks. By surfacing weak signals and providing context for deeper analysis, UEBA helps threat hunters connect the dots and uncover threats that might otherwise remain hidden.

In addition to user behavior, UEBA also analyzes the behavior of entities such as devices, applications, servers, and service accounts. This entity-level analysis is crucial in environments with large volumes of machine-generated activity. For example, a service account that suddenly initiates network scans or makes unexpected changes to system configurations may indicate a compromised script or automated attack. UEBA tracks these entities over time, comparing their behavior to historical norms and identifying deviations that suggest compromise. This allows organizations to detect threats in areas that are typically difficult to monitor with traditional tools.

Despite its strengths, UEBA is not without challenges. It requires significant data collection, storage, and processing capabilities to build and maintain accurate behavior models. Integrating data from multiple sources such as endpoint telemetry, network logs, authentication records, and cloud activity is necessary for full context, but can be complex and resource-intensive. Additionally, machine learning models must be carefully trained and tuned to avoid overwhelming analysts with false positives or missing subtle threats. Organizations must also ensure privacy and compliance when monitoring user behavior, striking a balance between security and employee trust.

The effectiveness of UEBA depends heavily on the quality of the underlying data and the maturity of the organization's security operations. In environments with poor visibility, inconsistent logging, or limited telemetry, behavior analytics may produce unreliable results. Conversely, in well-instrumented environments with comprehensive logging and strong data governance, UEBA can provide transformative insights that elevate the effectiveness of security programs. As organizations continue to adopt cloud services, remote work, and decentralized architectures, the importance of understanding behavior in context will only increase.

User and Entity Behavior Analytics enhances EDR by delivering a deeper understanding of how users and systems behave under normal conditions and how deviations from these patterns can signal risk. It enables the detection of threats that are often missed by traditional tools and provides the intelligence needed to respond with precision. As attackers continue to evolve, leveraging stolen credentials, living-off-the-land techniques, and insider access, behavior analytics offers a crucial layer of detection that adapts to modern threat scenarios. When integrated into a broader security strategy, UEBA not only strengthens threat detection and response but also supports risk management, compliance, and operational resilience.

EDR in a Zero Trust Framework

The concept of Zero Trust has reshaped the modern approach to cybersecurity, replacing the outdated perimeter-based defense model with one that assumes no implicit trust, regardless of whether a user or device is inside or outside the network. In a Zero Trust architecture, every access request must be continuously verified, and access is granted based on strict identity validation, device health checks, contextual awareness, and dynamic policy enforcement. Endpoint

Detection and Response plays a critical role in enabling and reinforcing the principles of Zero Trust by providing the necessary visibility, control, and response capabilities at the endpoint level, where users interact with data and where many attacks originate or culminate.

The traditional security model operated on the assumption that anything inside the network perimeter was trustworthy. Once authenticated, users and devices were often given broad access to resources. This model has proven insufficient in a landscape defined by remote work, cloud adoption, mobile devices, and advanced persistent threats. Zero Trust counters this by shifting the focus from network location to identity, behavior, and device posture. EDR systems, as instruments of continuous monitoring and enforcement, support this shift by delivering endpoint-level intelligence that confirms whether a device or user is acting in accordance with expected norms and policies.

EDR tools are uniquely positioned to support the Zero Trust mandate of continuous verification. They collect detailed telemetry from endpoints, including process activity, network connections, user actions, file access, and system modifications. This data is used not only to detect threats but also to evaluate the current security posture of the device. In a Zero Trust framework, access decisions are based in part on real-time assessments of endpoint health and behavior. If an endpoint shows signs of compromise, non-compliance with security policies, or anomalous behavior, it can be flagged, isolated, or denied access altogether. EDR provides the real-time insight necessary to make these determinations effectively.

Another core principle of Zero Trust is least-privilege access. Users and systems should only have the minimum level of access required to perform their duties. EDR supports this principle by identifying privilege escalation attempts, unauthorized access to sensitive data, and lateral movement within the network. These behaviors often signal attempts by adversaries to bypass access controls or escalate privileges once inside an environment. By monitoring for these indicators at the endpoint level, EDR systems help enforce least-privilege policies and prevent unauthorized expansion of access within the network.

Micro-segmentation is also central to the Zero Trust model. It involves dividing the network into smaller zones and enforcing granular access controls between them. While micro-segmentation is primarily implemented through network technologies, EDR complements it by monitoring and controlling how endpoints interact with different segments. For instance, an EDR system can detect when a device in one segment attempts to access resources in another segment without proper authorization. It can then alert security teams, trigger automated responses, or block the action entirely. In this way, EDR helps enforce micro-segmentation policies and provides the visibility needed to assess their effectiveness.

Identity and access management are foundational to Zero Trust, and EDR systems strengthen these functions by providing contextual data that supports authentication decisions. EDR can track which users are logged into which devices, monitor how credentials are used, and detect anomalies such as simultaneous logins from geographically distant locations or usage of high-privilege accounts in unusual contexts. These insights can be shared with identity providers and access control systems to enhance authentication processes. For example, if an EDR platform detects suspicious behavior from a device, it can inform the identity provider to challenge the user with multi-factor authentication or restrict access entirely. This bidirectional integration between EDR and identity systems ensures that authentication decisions are informed by the latest threat and behavior data.

In addition to supporting access decisions, EDR platforms enforce Zero Trust principles through automated containment and response. When an endpoint is determined to be risky or compromised, the EDR system can automatically isolate it from the rest of the network. This isolation prevents the attacker from moving laterally or exfiltrating data, aligning with the Zero Trust goal of minimizing the blast radius of a breach. Unlike traditional responses that might rely on manual intervention or broad network controls, EDR enables precise, device-level containment that supports business continuity while protecting critical assets.

The integration of EDR with Security Information and Event Management systems and Security Orchestration, Automation, and

Response platforms further amplifies its role in a Zero Trust framework. These integrations enable the correlation of endpoint data with other sources of telemetry, such as network logs, cloud activity, and identity events. They also allow for automated playbooks that orchestrate responses across the environment. For example, if an EDR system detects malware on an endpoint, it can trigger a coordinated response that includes revoking the user's session, blocking the device at the firewall, notifying the incident response team, and launching a forensic investigation. This kind of coordinated defense is essential in a Zero Trust model, where the assumption is that breaches are inevitable and rapid containment is critical.

Zero Trust also emphasizes the need for visibility and auditability. Organizations must be able to track who accessed what, from where, when, and under what conditions. EDR provides detailed logs of endpoint activity that support compliance reporting, forensic analysis, and continuous monitoring. These logs help organizations demonstrate that they are enforcing access policies, detecting violations, and responding effectively to incidents. In regulated industries, this capability is especially important for maintaining compliance with standards such as HIPAA, GDPR, and ISO 27001.

Behavioral analysis is another area where EDR enhances Zero Trust security. By building profiles of normal behavior for users and devices, EDR systems can detect deviations that suggest insider threats, compromised accounts, or advanced attacks. This aligns with the Zero Trust requirement for continuous risk assessment. Instead of relying on static rules or binary access decisions, EDR contributes to dynamic risk scoring that adjusts access levels in real time based on observed behavior. This adaptive security model ensures that access is always proportionate to the current risk level.

As organizations continue to adopt Zero Trust principles, EDR systems will become even more integral to enforcing policy, maintaining visibility, and enabling automated response. Their ability to monitor endpoints continuously, assess device health, detect anomalies, and orchestrate containment actions makes them indispensable in a security model that assumes no trust and demands verification at every step. By integrating closely with identity systems, access controls, and network segmentation strategies, EDR platforms provide the endpoint intelligence and enforcement mechanisms necessary to make Zero Trust both practical and effective. As threats evolve and the attack surface continues to expand, the synergy between EDR and Zero Trust will be essential for building resilient, adaptive, and secure digital environments.

Compliance and Regulatory Considerations

As cyber threats continue to grow in complexity and frequency, regulatory bodies around the world have implemented strict compliance standards to ensure organizations take proactive steps to protect sensitive data and maintain robust security postures. These compliance frameworks are designed to enforce accountability, ensure transparency, and establish consistent practices in how data is handled, monitored, and secured. Endpoint Detection and Response solutions play a pivotal role in helping organizations meet these regulatory obligations by offering visibility, control, and forensic capabilities that align with the technical and procedural requirements of various compliance regimes. The integration of EDR into a compliance strategy ensures that organizations are not only capable of detecting and responding to threats, but also of demonstrating due diligence and adherence to applicable laws.

Compliance regulations vary by industry, geography, and the nature of the data being handled, but many share core principles such as data protection, access control, auditability, incident response, and breach notification. Standards like the General Data Protection Regulation in the European Union, the Health Insurance Portability and Accountability Act in the United States, and the Payment Card Industry Data Security Standard require organizations to implement comprehensive security controls and maintain audit trails of user and system activity. EDR platforms contribute to these goals by continuously monitoring endpoint activity, capturing detailed logs, and generating real-time alerts that help identify potential violations or breaches.

One of the most direct ways EDR supports compliance is by enabling robust incident detection and response. Most regulatory frameworks mandate that organizations have the ability to identify and respond to security incidents in a timely manner. EDR systems provide this capability by detecting anomalies, generating alerts, and supporting rapid containment actions such as endpoint isolation or process termination. These tools allow security teams to quickly investigate suspicious activity and take corrective measures, helping the organization remain within the mandated incident response timelines and reporting windows. In some cases, regulations require breach notification within a specific timeframe, such as 72 hours, and the forensic data collected by EDR systems is essential for assessing the impact and scope of an incident accurately.

Data protection is another critical aspect of compliance, especially when it comes to safeguarding personally identifiable information, payment data, or protected health information. EDR tools help protect data by monitoring access patterns, detecting unauthorized file transfers, and identifying attempts to exfiltrate sensitive information. When configured properly, these systems can enforce data access policies and alert administrators when users or applications deviate from expected behavior. This aligns with the principle of data minimization and access control found in many regulatory texts, which require that only authorized individuals have access to sensitive data and only for legitimate business purposes.

Auditability and recordkeeping are essential elements of most compliance standards. Organizations must be able to produce logs and evidence that show how data was accessed, when security events occurred, and what actions were taken in response. EDR systems automatically generate comprehensive logs that include process activity, user behavior, file changes, and network connections. These logs can be stored securely and retrieved on demand for audits, investigations, or regulatory inquiries. The ability to produce these records quickly and accurately can be a determining factor in the outcome of compliance assessments or legal proceedings.

Another key consideration is the alignment of EDR practices with privacy regulations, especially in regions where data protection laws place strict limits on monitoring and data retention. Organizations must ensure that their use of EDR tools does not violate user privacy or result in unauthorized data collection. This requires careful configuration of telemetry settings, clear policies on data access, and transparent communication with employees and stakeholders. Data collected by EDR platforms must be secured both in transit and at rest, and retention policies must align with legal requirements. In some jurisdictions, organizations must also conduct data protection impact assessments before deploying monitoring tools, which includes evaluating the necessity, proportionality, and safeguards associated with EDR use.

Regulations such as ISO 27001 and NIST Cybersecurity Framework emphasize risk management and continuous improvement. EDR platforms contribute to these objectives by providing real-time insight into emerging threats and vulnerabilities, helping organizations adjust their risk posture dynamically. They also support ongoing improvement by offering metrics and reporting capabilities that track detection rates, response times, and the effectiveness of security controls. These metrics can be used to demonstrate progress in security maturity and to support internal governance and board-level reporting. In regulated industries, the ability to show that controls are not only in place but also regularly evaluated and improved is essential for maintaining certification and avoiding penalties.

Organizations operating in multiple jurisdictions must also consider the complexity of overlapping regulations. A single EDR deployment may need to satisfy the requirements of multiple regulatory bodies, each with its own definitions of sensitive data, breach thresholds, and compliance obligations. This adds a layer of complexity to configuration and policy management, requiring that EDR systems be flexible enough to accommodate varying data retention rules, alert thresholds, and logging requirements. Global organizations must ensure that data collected from endpoints in one region does not violate the laws of another, particularly when data is transmitted across borders or stored in centralized locations.

Compliance is not a one-time exercise but an ongoing process that requires constant vigilance and adaptation. The threat landscape evolves rapidly, and so do the expectations of regulators. EDR systems must therefore be regularly updated to recognize new threat signatures, behaviors, and tactics. Security teams must ensure that policies and playbooks are aligned with current compliance requirements and that any changes to infrastructure or business operations are reflected in their EDR configurations. Periodic reviews, tabletop exercises, and simulated incidents help test the readiness of EDR systems and ensure that they continue to support compliance objectives effectively.

The human element is equally important in ensuring compliance. EDR tools must be operated by trained professionals who understand not only the technical aspects of threat detection and response but also the legal and ethical considerations of data handling. Security teams must be aware of which actions are permissible under the applicable regulations, when notifications are required, and how to communicate incidents to stakeholders and authorities. Training and awareness programs are essential for ensuring that EDR-related practices are consistent, defensible, and aligned with the broader compliance strategy.

Endpoint Detection and Response systems are indispensable tools for organizations seeking to meet and maintain compliance in an increasingly regulated digital environment. By offering real-time monitoring, detailed audit trails, rapid response capabilities, and integration with broader governance frameworks, EDR platforms help bridge the gap between security operations and regulatory expectations. Their role extends beyond technical defense to include legal, ethical, and procedural dimensions of data protection and risk management. As compliance requirements continue to evolve, the adaptability and comprehensiveness of EDR solutions will remain vital in helping organizations navigate the complex intersection of cybersecurity and regulation.

EDR Deployment Best Practices

Deploying an Endpoint Detection and Response solution is a strategic initiative that requires careful planning, cross-functional collaboration, and continuous optimization. Unlike traditional antivirus software that can be deployed with minimal integration and configuration, EDR platforms are deeply embedded into the security operations framework and must interact seamlessly with other systems, including SIEMs, identity management platforms, and incident response tools. A successful deployment ensures maximum visibility across endpoints, minimizes false positives, and establishes a foundation for rapid and effective response to threats. To achieve these outcomes, organizations must follow best practices that consider not just the technical aspects of deployment, but also the operational, procedural, and cultural factors that influence the effectiveness of the solution.

The deployment process begins with a clear understanding of the organization's security objectives and the role EDR is expected to play. Whether the primary goal is to detect advanced persistent threats, reduce dwell time, achieve compliance, or improve incident response capabilities, defining success criteria is essential. These objectives will inform the configuration of detection rules, the integration with other systems, and the allocation of resources for monitoring and response. Early alignment between stakeholders from security, IT operations, compliance, and executive leadership ensures that expectations are realistic and that the deployment is supported across the organization.

A foundational step in EDR deployment is conducting a comprehensive asset inventory. EDR agents must be installed on all relevant endpoints, including workstations, laptops, servers, and virtual machines, across on-premises and remote environments. Without full visibility into the endpoint landscape, gaps in coverage can leave blind spots where threats can hide undetected. Inventory should include details such as device type, operating system, location, and criticality to the business. This information helps prioritize deployment, assess risk, and configure policies according to the specific characteristics of each asset class. It also enables organizations to ensure licensing is aligned with actual usage and that agents are deployed efficiently without duplicating effort.

Once endpoints are identified, organizations must plan the rollout of EDR agents in a staged and controlled manner. Starting with a pilot deployment on a representative subset of systems allows security teams to validate functionality, measure performance impact, and fine-tune policies before scaling up. The pilot group should include endpoints from different business units, geographies, and use cases to simulate the diversity of the environment. Feedback from this phase should be used to adjust configurations, address compatibility issues, and develop documentation and training materials. A phased rollout approach helps minimize disruption and builds confidence among users and administrators as the solution is expanded.

Agent configuration is a critical aspect of deployment and should be tailored to the organization's risk tolerance and operational requirements. Detection policies must strike a balance between sensitivity and precision to avoid overwhelming analysts with false positives while ensuring that real threats are not missed. Some organizations may choose to operate the EDR in detection-only mode during initial deployment, using alerts for monitoring and tuning purposes before enabling automated response actions. This staged approach provides an opportunity to validate alert quality, calibrate behavioral baselines, and develop response playbooks without prematurely triggering containment actions that could disrupt business operations.

Integration with existing security infrastructure is another best practice that enhances the value of EDR. Feeding endpoint telemetry into a central SIEM allows for correlation with network, cloud, and application data, providing a unified view of threats across the environment. Integration with identity providers enables context-aware detections that link endpoint activity to user behavior, improving threat attribution and reducing investigation time. Automated response orchestration through SOAR platforms can streamline incident handling by triggering playbooks based on EDR alerts. These integrations must be tested thoroughly to ensure that data flows are accurate, timely, and secure, and that response actions do not conflict or create unintended consequences.

User awareness and training are essential to the success of EDR deployment. Employees must understand how the system works, what types of activity may trigger alerts, and how to report suspicious behavior. Security analysts and incident responders must be trained in the use of the EDR console, investigation tools, and response functions. Training should cover common use cases, alert triage, process analysis, and forensic data interpretation. Ongoing education ensures that the security team is capable of leveraging the full capabilities of the EDR platform and that users understand their role in supporting endpoint security.

Monitoring and continuous improvement are required to maintain the effectiveness of the EDR deployment. Threats evolve rapidly, and detection rules must be updated regularly to reflect new tactics, techniques, and procedures. Telemetry should be reviewed to identify changes in endpoint behavior, and detection models should be retrained to adapt to new normal patterns. Performance metrics such as detection accuracy, response time, and incident resolution rates should be tracked and used to guide optimization efforts. Feedback from investigations, audits, and red team exercises should inform refinements to policies, playbooks, and training programs.

Governance and policy alignment ensure that the EDR system operates within legal, ethical, and organizational boundaries. Policies must define acceptable use, data retention, access control, and escalation procedures. These policies should be reviewed regularly and aligned with regulatory requirements such as GDPR, HIPAA, or industry-specific standards. Access to EDR data and response functions should be restricted to authorized personnel based on the principle of least privilege. Audit logs should be maintained to provide accountability and support compliance reporting.

Finally, strong vendor collaboration supports long-term success. EDR vendors offer threat intelligence, best practice guidance, and technical support that can enhance the deployment. Engaging in regular briefings, product updates, and training opportunities helps organizations stay informed about emerging threats and new capabilities. Participation in user communities and knowledge exchanges can also provide valuable insights from peer organizations that have faced similar challenges.

A well-planned and executed EDR deployment enables organizations to detect and respond to threats more effectively, reduce risk, and strengthen their overall cybersecurity posture. By following best practices that encompass technical configuration, integration, training, and governance, organizations can ensure that their EDR solution delivers its full potential and remains a cornerstone of a resilient, adaptive, and proactive security strategy.

Securing Remote Endpoints and BYOD

The rise of remote work and the widespread adoption of Bring Your Own Device policies have significantly expanded the modern enterprise's attack surface. As organizations embrace flexibility and mobility to boost productivity and support a global workforce, they must also contend with the security challenges that come with managing endpoints outside the traditional network perimeter. Remote endpoints and personal devices operate in diverse environments, from home networks and public Wi-Fi to unmanaged locations across the world. This creates unique risks that require tailored strategies, robust visibility, and intelligent control mechanisms to ensure that organizational assets remain protected regardless of where or how users connect.

One of the most pressing challenges in securing remote endpoints is the lack of consistent network-level protections. In traditional enterprise settings, endpoints benefit from centralized controls such as firewalls, intrusion prevention systems, and network segmentation. These tools limit exposure to threats and provide an additional layer of defense even when endpoint security fails. Remote endpoints, by contrast, often operate in untrusted networks where these protective measures do not exist. Without perimeter defenses, the endpoint becomes the first and last line of defense, making Endpoint Detection and Response tools an essential component of remote security strategy.

Endpoint Detection and Response platforms offer real-time visibility into endpoint behavior, allowing security teams to monitor for malicious activity, detect anomalies, and respond to incidents regardless of the device's physical location. The telemetry collected by EDR systems includes process execution, file modifications, network activity, and user behavior, enabling organizations to identify threats such as ransomware, credential theft, and data exfiltration even on unmanaged or remote endpoints. EDR agents operate independently of network location, ensuring continuous protection and detection capabilities whether a user is in the office, at home, or traveling.

Bring Your Own Device environments introduce an additional layer of complexity. In BYOD scenarios, employees use their personal devices to access corporate resources, often without the same level of oversight or control that is applied to company-owned assets. These devices may lack essential security configurations, run outdated software, or host unauthorized applications that increase the risk of compromise. At the same time, organizations must respect user privacy and avoid intrusive monitoring that violates personal boundaries. This creates a delicate balance between securing corporate data and maintaining trust with users.

To address the risks of BYOD, organizations must implement clear policies that define acceptable use, security requirements, and device enrollment procedures. Devices that access corporate systems should be subject to minimum baseline controls, including endpoint protection, strong authentication, encryption, and automatic updates. EDR platforms designed for BYOD environments often include features such as lightweight agents, data segmentation, and contextual access controls. These capabilities ensure that sensitive data is isolated, monitored, and protected without compromising the personal use of the device. Integration with Mobile Device Management or Unified Endpoint Management platforms further enhances control by allowing administrators to enforce compliance policies, remotely wipe corporate data, and manage device posture assessments.

One of the key enablers of secure remote access is the use of identity-based controls and multi-factor authentication. Since network boundaries can no longer be relied upon to verify trust, authentication must be tied to the user's identity and the security posture of the device. EDR platforms contribute to this model by providing device risk scores based on observed behavior and security posture. These scores can be shared with identity providers and access management systems to make dynamic access decisions. For instance, if an endpoint exhibits suspicious activity or fails to meet compliance checks, access to corporate resources can be restricted until the issue is resolved.

Another important consideration in securing remote and BYOD endpoints is visibility. Security teams must be able to monitor all endpoints, regardless of where they are located or who owns them. This requires cloud-native EDR solutions that can scale globally, support diverse operating systems, and operate across different connectivity scenarios. Visibility must be consistent and continuous, allowing analysts to detect threats in real time and correlate activity across multiple endpoints. Without this level of insight, threats can go undetected, especially when attackers target endpoints that are temporarily disconnected from the corporate network.

Remote endpoints are also more susceptible to social engineering attacks, such as phishing, since users may be more isolated and lack immediate support. EDR tools can help mitigate this risk by detecting malicious attachments, unusual process execution, and behavioral anomalies that indicate a compromised user or endpoint. By integrating with email security platforms, EDR systems can provide a comprehensive defense that begins with detection and continues through response, even when the initial vector is outside the endpoint itself.

Response capabilities are especially critical for remote environments, where physical access to the device may not be possible. EDR platforms must provide remote remediation options, such as process termination, file quarantine, and device isolation, to allow security teams to contain threats without delay. These actions can be initiated automatically based on detection policies or triggered manually through the EDR console. Remote forensics capabilities enable analysts to investigate incidents without retrieving the device, using telemetry and live data collection to understand what occurred and how to respond.

Data protection is another core challenge when securing remote and BYOD endpoints. Sensitive data must be protected against unauthorized access, theft, or leakage, regardless of where it resides. EDR systems contribute by monitoring data access patterns, detecting unauthorized transfers, and enforcing data loss prevention rules. Combined with encryption and secure access controls, this creates a multi-layered defense that ensures data confidentiality and integrity across all endpoint types.

Finally, user education plays a crucial role in securing remote and BYOD endpoints. Users must understand the risks associated with remote work and personal device usage, as well as the security policies and tools in place to protect them. Awareness programs should include training on recognizing phishing attempts, securing home networks, managing passwords, and complying with corporate security guidelines. When users are informed and engaged, they become active participants in the organization's security posture rather than passive risk factors.

Securing remote endpoints and BYOD devices requires a holistic approach that combines technology, policy, and user engagement. EDR platforms provide the foundation for visibility, detection, and response, enabling organizations to maintain control over a dispersed and dynamic endpoint landscape. By aligning EDR capabilities with access controls, data protection strategies, and user training, organizations can manage the risks of remote work and personal device usage without compromising flexibility or productivity. In an increasingly perimeter-less world, this approach ensures that endpoints remain secure, users stay protected, and business operations continue without disruption.

Agent-Based vs Agentless EDR Approaches

Endpoint Detection and Response platforms are central to modern cybersecurity strategies, offering the visibility and control needed to detect, investigate, and respond to threats at the endpoint level. A key architectural decision that organizations must make when implementing EDR solutions is whether to deploy agent-based or agentless approaches. Each model offers unique advantages and trade-offs, and understanding the differences between them is essential to selecting the most appropriate strategy for a given environment. The debate between agent-based and agentless EDR is not about which is universally better, but rather which aligns best with an organization's infrastructure, risk profile, operational needs, and compliance requirements.

Agent-based EDR relies on a small software component installed directly on each endpoint. This agent continuously collects telemetry such as process activity, file changes, network connections, and user behavior. It may also enforce policies, block malicious actions, isolate compromised systems, and execute response commands. The agent operates in real time and provides deep visibility into endpoint behavior, often including kernel-level events and memory operations. This comprehensive data collection enables rapid detection of advanced threats and supports detailed forensic investigations. Because the agent runs locally, it can perform tasks even when the endpoint is offline or disconnected from the corporate network, syncing with the central management console once reconnected.

One of the key strengths of agent-based EDR is its ability to provide granular telemetry that is often unavailable through agentless means. For example, detecting reflective DLL injection, process hollowing, or manipulation of registry keys typically requires access to the operating system at a privileged level. Agent-based tools can achieve this access and deliver high-fidelity insights into both malicious behavior and system state. Additionally, agent-based systems can execute actions directly on the endpoint, such as quarantining files, killing processes, or applying remediation scripts. This real-time control is critical for immediate response and containment of fast-moving threats like ransomware.

However, agent-based EDR also introduces certain challenges. Deploying and maintaining agents across a diverse and distributed environment can be resource-intensive. Compatibility issues with legacy systems, virtual machines, or specialized hardware may arise. Organizations must also manage updates, patches, and potential performance impacts on the endpoints themselves. In environments with strict regulatory constraints or limited administrative access, installing agents may not be feasible or permissible. Furthermore, the presence of an agent can be detected by sophisticated attackers, who may attempt to disable or evade it as part of their attack chain. To mitigate this risk, agents must be hardened, tamper-resistant, and monitored continuously for signs of manipulation.

In contrast, agentless EDR solutions collect endpoint data without installing software directly on the device. These platforms typically rely on existing infrastructure such as network traffic analysis, log aggregation, cloud APIs, or remote access protocols to monitor and manage endpoints. For example, in cloud environments, agentless EDR tools may leverage native telemetry from infrastructure-as-a-service platforms to monitor virtual machines and workloads. In on-premises networks, agentless systems might pull data from Active Directory, Sysmon logs, or endpoint management platforms. This approach reduces deployment complexity and overhead, making it attractive for environments where scalability, speed, and ease of implementation are critical.

Agentless EDR is particularly well-suited for cloud-native environments, where endpoints are often ephemeral, highly dynamic, and orchestrated through automation. In such settings, installing and maintaining agents on short-lived instances may not be practical. Agentless tools can quickly discover new assets, assess their security posture, and collect telemetry using platform-native APIs or log streaming services. This provides visibility across the entire cloud infrastructure without requiring persistent software installations. Agentless solutions also offer value in environments with heterogeneous systems or devices that do not support agent installation, such as printers, IoT devices, or certain industrial control systems.

Despite these advantages, agentless EDR has limitations in terms of depth and immediacy. Because it relies on external data sources, it may miss real-time events or low-level system activity. The granularity of detection is often dependent on the fidelity and timeliness of the underlying data, which can vary significantly across platforms. Agentless tools may struggle to detect sophisticated attacks that reside entirely in memory, manipulate internal APIs, or exploit kernel-level vulnerabilities. They also typically lack the capability to take immediate, local response actions such as process termination or system isolation, which can delay containment efforts during active incidents.

Another consideration is network dependency. Agentless solutions often require continuous connectivity to central log sources, APIs, or control planes to function effectively. If connectivity is disrupted, data collection and visibility may be delayed or interrupted. This is less of a concern in agent-based systems, where local agents can continue to operate independently and sync later. Additionally, agentless systems may depend on elevated credentials to access data or perform actions remotely, introducing potential risks if those credentials are compromised. Managing these access controls securely and monitoring for misuse is critical in maintaining a secure agentless deployment.

In many cases, organizations benefit from a hybrid approach that leverages the strengths of both models. Agent-based EDR can be deployed on high-value assets, critical endpoints, and systems where detailed monitoring and response are essential. Agentless EDR can complement this by extending visibility to devices where agents cannot be installed or where lightweight, rapid coverage is needed. This blended strategy allows for comprehensive coverage across a wide range of devices and environments while balancing performance, complexity, and risk. It also supports more agile operations by enabling security teams to scale monitoring and response across different infrastructure types, from traditional desktops and servers to virtual machines and cloud workloads.

Ultimately, the choice between agent-based and agentless EDR should be guided by a thorough assessment of organizational needs, endpoint diversity, threat landscape, and compliance obligations. Each model offers distinct benefits and trade-offs that must be weighed carefully. By understanding the strengths and limitations of both approaches, organizations can design a security architecture that provides robust endpoint protection, effective incident response, and the flexibility to adapt as technology and threats evolve. Whether deploying agents for deep inspection or leveraging agentless tools for broad coverage, the goal remains the same: to secure endpoints effectively and maintain operational integrity in a dynamic digital environment.

Endpoint Visibility and Inventory Management

In the realm of cybersecurity, endpoint visibility and inventory management form the foundation upon which effective threat detection, response, and control are built. Without full visibility into every device that connects to the organization's infrastructure, security teams are left blind to potential risks and unable to enforce consistent policies. As endpoints continue to proliferate in the form of workstations, laptops, servers, virtual machines, mobile devices, and Internet of Things assets, maintaining a real-time, accurate inventory has become both more challenging and more critical. Organizations that fail to manage their endpoint landscape with precision risk leaving unmonitored devices exposed, making them ideal entry points for attackers and sources of data leakage.

Endpoint visibility refers to the ability to identify, monitor, and assess every endpoint connected to the network. This includes not just the devices themselves, but also the activities performed on them, the users operating them, and the applications they run. Visibility allows security teams to understand the environment in its entirety, detect anomalous behavior, and respond appropriately to incidents. Without this level of insight, an organization cannot effectively enforce its security policies, measure its attack surface, or identify unauthorized or rogue devices. Endpoint Detection and Response solutions play a key role in enabling visibility by deploying agents or leveraging agentless integrations to gather telemetry from endpoints across the enterprise.

Comprehensive visibility begins with the creation and maintenance of an accurate asset inventory. Inventory management is not simply a list of known devices, but a dynamic and continuously updated database of all endpoints, complete with contextual attributes such as operating system, hardware specifications, installed software, patch levels, user identities, geographic location, and network connections. This information allows organizations to classify assets by criticality, risk level, and compliance status, enabling more effective prioritization and incident response. A static inventory quickly becomes outdated and unreliable, especially in modern environments where new devices are added, removed, or reconfigured on a daily basis.

The challenge of maintaining real-time visibility is compounded by the rise of remote work, cloud services, and BYOD policies. Devices may connect from various locations, networks, and domains, and may only be intermittently visible to traditional network-based asset discovery tools. Endpoint Detection and Response systems address this gap by maintaining persistent connections to managed devices and reporting telemetry back to a central console, regardless of the device's physical location. This capability is essential for ensuring that all endpoints are monitored and accounted for, even when they operate outside the perimeter or in unmanaged networks.

Automated discovery is a critical feature of modern EDR platforms that supports visibility and inventory accuracy. Through active scanning, integration with directory services, or leveraging existing IT asset management systems, EDR tools can identify new endpoints as they appear and begin collecting data immediately. Some platforms offer real-time discovery of unmanaged devices and provide workflows for bringing them under management or flagging them as unauthorized. This proactive approach helps security teams close gaps in coverage and prevents shadow IT from introducing unknown risks into the environment.

Visibility also extends to software and application inventory. Knowing what software is installed, running, or being used on each endpoint is essential for managing vulnerabilities, licensing, and compliance. EDR platforms often include capabilities to track installed applications, monitor execution behavior, and detect unauthorized or risky software. This allows organizations to enforce application whitelisting, detect the use of unapproved tools, and identify indicators of compromise such as the installation of known malicious binaries. By correlating software usage with endpoint behavior, security teams can uncover advanced threats that rely on legitimate tools, also known as living-off-the-land techniques.

Another vital dimension of endpoint visibility is user context. Understanding who is using a device, what privileges they have, and how they are interacting with systems adds depth to security monitoring. EDR solutions enrich telemetry with user information from identity providers and authentication systems, linking actions to individuals and enabling detection of abnormal behavior. This user-centric approach supports insider threat detection, policy enforcement, and compliance auditing. It also helps distinguish between human error and malicious intent, providing context that is crucial during investigations.

Real-time visibility supports effective incident response by providing immediate access to endpoint state and history. When an alert is triggered, responders need to understand what happened before, during, and after the event to assess the impact and determine appropriate actions. EDR platforms maintain rich historical data that allows analysts to reconstruct timelines, trace attacker movements, and identify affected systems. The ability to query this data quickly and correlate it with other sources such as SIEM logs or threat intelligence accelerates investigations and supports accurate root cause analysis.

Visibility and inventory management are also essential for compliance with regulatory standards and frameworks. Many regulations require organizations to maintain accurate asset records, enforce access controls, monitor endpoint activity, and demonstrate accountability. EDR solutions provide the logging, reporting, and audit capabilities needed to meet these requirements. They also help organizations prove the presence of compensating controls, document incident response procedures, and support forensic investigations. In regulated industries such as healthcare, finance, and critical infrastructure, failure to maintain endpoint visibility can result in non-compliance, fines, or legal liability.

To ensure visibility translates into actionable security outcomes, organizations must integrate inventory data into broader security and IT operations. This includes feeding endpoint data into vulnerability management programs to prioritize patching efforts, aligning asset information with configuration management databases, and using endpoint insights to inform access control decisions. Collaboration between IT, security, and compliance teams is essential to ensure that asset data is accurate, accessible, and aligned with organizational priorities. Automation can assist by synchronizing inventory records across platforms, triggering alerts for unauthorized changes, and enforcing policies consistently.

Visibility is not a one-time achievement but an ongoing process that must evolve with the environment. As new technologies emerge, organizational structures change, and threats become more sophisticated, the tools and processes used to manage endpoints must be continuously refined. Regular audits, asset discovery scans, and integration checks are necessary to maintain confidence in the visibility framework. Metrics such as asset coverage, detection rate, and response time help measure effectiveness and identify areas for improvement.

Endpoint visibility and inventory management are fundamental to building a resilient security architecture. They enable organizations to detect threats earlier, respond more effectively, and manage risk with precision. EDR platforms provide the tools needed to maintain visibility across a diverse and dynamic landscape, ensuring that no device goes unmonitored and no threat goes undetected. In a world where endpoints are the frontline of digital interaction, the ability to see, understand, and manage every asset is not just a best practice—it is a necessity for securing the enterprise.

Operationalizing Threat Hunting with EDR

Threat hunting is an advanced cybersecurity practice that involves proactively searching for signs of malicious activity within an environment before alerts are triggered or damage occurs. Unlike traditional detection methods that rely on predefined rules or known signatures, threat hunting is hypothesis-driven and centered on uncovering unknown threats that evade standard security controls. Operationalizing threat hunting means transforming it from an occasional, ad hoc activity into a repeatable, strategic function within the security operations framework. Endpoint Detection and Response platforms serve as a foundational tool in this process, providing the telemetry, investigative capabilities, and automation required to scale and embed threat hunting into daily security operations.

The first step in operationalizing threat hunting with EDR is establishing the necessary visibility. EDR platforms collect rich telemetry from endpoints, including process execution, file modifications, network communications, registry changes, user activity, and memory usage. This data enables hunters to form hypotheses based on behavioral anomalies and patterns that might indicate the presence of adversaries. Without this visibility, threat hunting efforts are reduced to guesswork. EDR ensures that even subtle and stealthy behaviors are captured and made accessible for analysis, creating a data-rich environment where hunters can explore various angles of potential compromise.

A critical enabler of operationalized threat hunting is the development of repeatable methodologies. Rather than relying on the intuition of individual analysts, mature threat hunting programs document procedures, standardize workflows, and build knowledge repositories that guide new investigations. These procedures often begin with a hypothesis such as an attacker using legitimate remote access tools for lateral movement or a compromised account accessing sensitive data outside of business hours. Using the EDR platform, analysts can query endpoint data to look for evidence supporting or refuting the hypothesis. If signs of compromise are found, the hunt may evolve into an incident response process. If not, the findings can still inform the refinement of detection rules and enrich the threat intelligence repository.

EDR tools enable efficient and scalable threat hunting by offering powerful search and query capabilities. Analysts can pivot through datasets using keyword searches, behavioral filters, and custom scripts to identify suspicious indicators. For instance, a hunter may search for endpoints that launched command-line tools from unusual directories or ran scripts containing base64-encoded payloads. These queries can span hundreds or thousands of endpoints simultaneously, reducing the time needed to identify potential threats. More advanced EDR platforms support hunt automation by allowing hunters to save and reuse queries, schedule searches, and even integrate with external threat intelligence sources for dynamic indicator matching.

Threat hunting with EDR is also enriched through behavioral baselining. By understanding what is normal in the environment, hunters can more easily identify outliers and investigate anomalies. EDR systems help establish these baselines by continuously monitoring endpoint behavior and highlighting deviations that may not necessarily trigger alerts but warrant further inspection. This approach is especially valuable for identifying living-off-the-land techniques, where attackers use legitimate tools like PowerShell, WMI, or scheduled tasks to blend in with normal operations. These techniques often go unnoticed by signature-based detection but become apparent when viewed through the lens of contextual behavioral analysis.

Collaboration is essential to scaling threat hunting beyond individual analysts. EDR platforms support this by enabling hunt data sharing, team-based tagging, and centralized investigation workspaces. Findings from a hunt can be documented, shared with detection engineering teams, and used to improve alert rules, enrich playbooks, and strengthen defenses across the organization. By operationalizing the feedback loop between hunters, responders, and detection engineers, organizations create a system of continuous improvement that enhances threat detection and response capabilities over time.

Metrics play an important role in operationalizing threat hunting. By measuring indicators such as dwell time reduction, number of hunts conducted, percentage of hunts leading to detections, and improvement in mean time to respond, organizations can evaluate the effectiveness of their program. EDR platforms often provide dashboards and reporting features that track hunt activity and support performance assessments. These insights help justify investment in hunting programs, identify areas for additional training, and drive resource allocation.

Operationalized threat hunting must also include a focus on adversary emulation and hypothesis generation. Using frameworks like MITRE ATT&CK, hunters can map out potential adversary behaviors and tactics, guiding their efforts to areas of the kill chain that are relevant to current threat intelligence. EDR data allows analysts to simulate how an attacker might behave in the environment and test whether those behaviors would be visible or missed. By emulating known threats and exploring unknown scenarios, hunting becomes both a detection exercise and a resilience assessment.

Training and skill development are crucial for the long-term success of an operational threat hunting program. Analysts must be proficient not only in the use of EDR tools but also in understanding operating system internals, malware behavior, scripting, and attacker tradecraft. EDR platforms that offer rich telemetry, intuitive interfaces, and integrated learning resources empower hunters to develop expertise more rapidly. Moreover, simulated hunts, capture-the-flag exercises, and red team engagements help sharpen skills and expose analysts to real-world scenarios that enhance their investigative instincts.

To maintain operational momentum, threat hunting should be incorporated into the daily rhythm of the security operations center. This includes allocating dedicated time for hunts, aligning hunts with strategic threat intelligence, and integrating hunt findings into detection engineering. Security leaders must support the effort by providing the necessary time, tools, and recognition to ensure that hunting is seen not as a luxury but as an integral part of proactive defense. Regularly scheduled hunts focused on high-risk areas, such as domain controllers, executive endpoints, or third-party software, help identify weak spots and drive mitigation efforts before they can be exploited.

Finally, the integration of threat hunting with response automation enhances its operational impact. When hunt findings reveal valid threats, EDR platforms can initiate automated containment actions such as isolating the endpoint, killing processes, or blocking network connections. These automated responses reduce the time between detection and remediation, especially in environments where threats spread quickly. Automation also ensures consistency in response and allows hunting teams to focus on higher-value analytical work instead of routine containment.

Operationalizing threat hunting with EDR transforms cybersecurity from a reactive discipline into a proactive one. It empowers organizations to detect and respond to threats that evade traditional defenses, enhances situational awareness, and builds institutional knowledge that strengthens overall resilience. Through visibility, methodology, collaboration, and automation, EDR becomes more than just a tool—it becomes the engine that drives continuous discovery, detection, and defense across the entire endpoint landscape. As attackers evolve and adapt, the ability to hunt, learn, and respond must be embedded into the core fabric of security operations. Threat hunting, when fully operationalized, is not an isolated task but a perpetual function that defines the maturity and agility of a truly resilient cybersecurity program.

Role of MITRE ATT&CK in EDR Strategy

The MITRE ATT&CK framework has emerged as one of the most transformative tools in the field of cybersecurity, particularly when applied to Endpoint Detection and Response strategies. ATT&CK, which stands for Adversarial Tactics, Techniques, and Common Knowledge, provides a globally accessible knowledge base of adversary behavior, structured around real-world observations and intelligence. Rather than focusing on specific indicators such as IP addresses or file hashes, the framework categorizes adversary actions according to the tactics they serve and the techniques they employ. This behavioral approach aligns seamlessly with the goals and capabilities of modern EDR platforms, which are designed to monitor endpoint activity, detect anomalies, and respond to suspicious behavior in real time. Integrating the MITRE ATT&CK framework into EDR strategy enhances detection accuracy, improves response workflows, and fosters a more proactive and informed approach to cyber defense.

At the core of the MITRE ATT&CK framework is a matrix that maps the lifecycle of a cyberattack from initial access to execution, persistence, privilege escalation, defense evasion, credential access, discovery, lateral movement, collection, command and control, exfiltration, and impact. Each tactic represents a phase of the attacker's objective, while the techniques under each tactic describe the specific ways that objective may be achieved. EDR solutions, when mapped against this matrix, become tools not just for detecting isolated incidents but for understanding how threats unfold over time. By tracking behavior across multiple techniques and tactics, analysts can piece together a coherent picture of an adversary's activity, which is vital for containment, eradication, and future prevention.

In practical terms, the MITRE ATT&CK framework enables EDR platforms to enhance their detection capabilities through behavior-based logic. Traditional security controls often rely on signature-based detection, which can fail when attackers use novel malware or legitimate tools in unexpected ways. ATT&CK shifts the focus from the tools to the behaviors, allowing EDR systems to flag suspicious activity based on how it is executed rather than what is executed. For example, instead of only detecting a known malicious binary, an EDR solution informed by ATT&CK may flag the use of PowerShell for process injection, recognizing the technique regardless of the specific command used. This approach increases the resilience of detection capabilities against evasion techniques and zero-day threats.

Another advantage of incorporating MITRE ATT&CK into EDR strategy is the standardization it brings to threat detection and analysis. The common language provided by the framework allows different teams within an organization—such as threat hunters, incident responders, and detection engineers—to communicate findings and strategies using a consistent taxonomy. This consistency also extends to reporting and compliance, where organizations can describe incidents and detection coverage in terms that are universally recognized across the cybersecurity community. It enhances collaboration not only internally but also externally with vendors, industry partners, and threat intelligence providers who adopt the same framework to describe threats and mitigations.

MITRE ATT&CK also supports detection engineering by guiding the development and validation of detection rules. EDR platforms can be configured to detect specific ATT&CK techniques based on the telemetry they collect. For instance, the use of a tool like Mimikatz to dump credentials can be linked to the Credential Dumping technique under the Credential Access tactic. Security teams can create detection logic that identifies this behavior regardless of how it is implemented, then test and refine those rules using simulated attacks. Many EDR vendors now offer built-in detection coverage maps that show which ATT&CK techniques are being monitored and where gaps may exist. This visual representation helps organizations prioritize improvements and assess their detection maturity.

Threat hunting is another area where the MITRE ATT&CK framework amplifies the value of EDR. Hunters can use the framework to generate hypotheses about how adversaries might behave in the environment and design their searches accordingly. For example, if intelligence suggests that a particular threat actor favors lateral movement via remote desktop protocols, a threat hunter can investigate endpoint data for unusual RDP sessions that align with that technique. The structured nature of ATT&CK allows hunters to focus their efforts, avoid redundancy, and build repeatable processes that can be shared and refined over time. EDR platforms support this effort by enabling deep and fast searches across endpoint telemetry, correlated with ATT&CK techniques.

Response operations also benefit from the integration of MITRE ATT&CK into EDR strategies. When an alert is generated, mapping it to a known ATT&CK technique provides immediate context about the adversary's intent and possible next steps. This contextual understanding helps responders make faster, more informed decisions about containment and remediation. If multiple alerts across different endpoints correspond to techniques under the same tactic, such as lateral movement, responders can infer that an attacker is attempting to spread and take appropriate action to isolate affected systems. EDR platforms with ATT&CK integration often provide visual kill chain representations that illustrate how an attack unfolded according to the framework, enhancing post-incident analysis and reporting.

The ATT&CK framework also plays a significant role in adversary emulation and red team exercises. Security teams can use it to design simulated attacks that mimic real-world adversaries, testing the organization's ability to detect and respond to those behaviors. EDR platforms that are aligned with ATT&CK can be evaluated based on their ability to detect the techniques used during these simulations. This approach supports continuous improvement and validation of detection capabilities, helping to ensure that security controls remain effective as threats evolve. Organizations can use the results of these exercises to refine their EDR configurations, update detection logic, and close coverage gaps identified during testing.

MITRE ATT&CK's influence extends to security metrics and program maturity assessments. Organizations can measure how much of the framework they currently monitor, how often specific techniques are detected, and how long it takes to respond to behaviors mapped to certain tactics. These metrics provide insight into strengths and weaknesses across the attack lifecycle and help inform investment decisions, staffing needs, and strategic priorities. Over time, organizations that operationalize ATT&CK within their EDR strategies develop a more comprehensive and adaptive approach to threat management, where detection and response are guided by knowledge of how adversaries operate, not just what tools they use.

Incorporating the MITRE ATT&CK framework into EDR strategy represents a shift from reactive to proactive security. It encourages organizations to think like adversaries, structure their defenses around real-world behaviors, and continuously assess their readiness to detect and respond to sophisticated attacks. EDR platforms empowered by ATT&CK not only improve technical detection capabilities but also drive better decision-making, collaboration, and situational awareness across the entire cybersecurity function. As adversaries continue to refine their methods and exploit new attack surfaces, the structured, behavior-focused approach championed by MITRE ATT&CK will remain a vital component of resilient and intelligent EDR strategies.

Threat Lifecycle and Kill Chain Mapping

Understanding the full lifecycle of a cyber threat is essential for building a resilient and effective security strategy. The concept of the threat lifecycle refers to the sequential phases an adversary follows when launching an attack, from initial reconnaissance to ultimate impact. Mapping these phases to a kill chain model allows security teams to dissect complex attacks, identify vulnerabilities in their defenses, and respond more effectively. The kill chain serves as a visual and conceptual framework that breaks down the steps an attacker takes to accomplish their objectives, providing insight into both their methods and their progression. Integrating threat lifecycle awareness and kill chain mapping into Endpoint Detection and Response strategy transforms raw alerts into actionable intelligence and enables security operations teams to anticipate, detect, and disrupt adversarial activity at multiple stages.

The kill chain model was originally developed by Lockheed Martin as a military concept and later adapted to cybersecurity. It includes distinct phases such as reconnaissance, weaponization, delivery, exploitation, installation, command and control, and actions on objectives. Each phase represents a specific goal the adversary must achieve in order to advance the attack. While different frameworks may vary slightly in terminology or structure, the essence remains consistent: understanding that cyberattacks are not single events, but rather complex sequences of interrelated steps. Mapping EDR-detected activity to the kill chain helps security teams understand where the attacker currently is within that sequence and what actions are likely to follow.

The reconnaissance phase is the earliest stage, during which attackers gather information about their target. This may involve scanning for vulnerabilities, identifying open ports, profiling employees through social media, or harvesting domain records. Although this phase occurs outside the endpoint in many cases, its results directly influence the attack path. Security teams may gain visibility into reconnaissance activity through suspicious web traffic, phishing attempts, or anomalies in DNS queries. While EDR tools may not directly detect the reconnaissance phase, they can play a crucial role in catching early delivery attempts that stem from it, especially if attackers attempt to validate targets via malware delivery.

The weaponization phase involves crafting a payload that can exploit a vulnerability or trick a user into enabling execution. This could be a malicious macro embedded in a Word document or a custom exploit designed to target a known flaw in a widely used application. EDR platforms are instrumental in detecting weaponization tactics by monitoring for known exploit patterns, identifying malicious document behavior, or recognizing file types and payloads commonly associated with weaponized content. Alerts generated during this phase often represent the adversary's first direct attempt at interacting with the environment.

Delivery is the point at which the attacker transmits the payload to the target system. Common delivery vectors include email attachments, malicious links, drive-by downloads, or USB devices. This is typically where EDR first comes into full effect. By monitoring the creation and execution of new files, analyzing command-line behavior, and integrating with email or web gateways, EDR tools can flag and block suspicious deliveries. Security teams can use kill chain mapping to correlate delivery events with weaponization indicators, establishing a timeline that helps determine whether the attack is part of a broader campaign.

Exploitation occurs when the delivered payload is executed, taking advantage of a vulnerability or tricking the user into granting elevated privileges or running malicious code. This phase is critical because it marks the transition from a potential threat to an active compromise. EDR solutions detect exploitation techniques by observing anomalous process behavior, exploit indicators such as memory corruption, or privilege escalation attempts. Kill chain mapping ensures that such alerts are not viewed in isolation but are connected to earlier phases, helping analysts recognize the broader attack structure and respond accordingly.

The installation phase involves the establishment of a persistent presence on the target system. This can include installing a remote access trojan, modifying the registry, creating scheduled tasks, or deploying rootkits. EDR platforms excel in detecting installation activity due to their ability to monitor file system changes, service creation, and persistence mechanisms. Detecting and interrupting the installation phase is critical because it limits the attacker's ability to regain access or pivot within the network. When mapped against the kill chain, these detections help identify compromised systems and enable security teams to execute targeted remediation.

Command and control, or C2, refers to the communication channel between the compromised endpoint and the attacker's infrastructure. This is where the attacker sends instructions and receives stolen data or reconnaissance results. EDR platforms provide visibility into network connections, DNS lookups, and process behavior that may indicate the presence of C2 activity. Anomalies such as beaconing to unusual IP addresses, encrypted communication over uncommon ports, or repetitive outbound traffic are all signs of C2 operations. Kill chain mapping reveals how this communication ties back to earlier exploitation and installation events, allowing for faster isolation of affected endpoints.

Finally, actions on objectives represent the attacker's end goal, whether that is data theft, system destruction, or lateral movement to other parts of the network. EDR tools track sensitive file access, unauthorized data transfers, lateral movement behaviors such as credential dumping or remote desktop activity, and changes to security configurations. The kill chain model helps contextualize these actions, highlighting how the attacker has progressed through the earlier phases and what patterns they have followed. This holistic understanding supports full attack remediation and post-incident analysis.

The value of kill chain mapping lies in its ability to turn fragmented alerts into a cohesive narrative. Instead of responding to individual events in isolation, security analysts can trace the entire trajectory of an attack and determine how far the adversary has advanced. This enables faster, more strategic response actions and enhances the quality of forensic investigations. It also helps identify weaknesses in existing controls. If an attacker reaches the C2 or exfiltration phases undetected, it suggests that earlier detection mechanisms may need reinforcement. By using kill chain mapping to review incidents, organizations can continuously improve their detection and response strategies.

Kill chain mapping is not limited to post-incident response. It can be operationalized within EDR platforms to enhance proactive defense. For example, alerts can be enriched with kill chain phase tags, enabling security teams to prioritize based on where an event falls in the lifecycle. Early-phase activity such as delivery or exploitation may trigger containment workflows, while later-stage activity may prompt immediate isolation and escalation. Integration with threat intelligence feeds mapped to kill chain phases further refines this approach, helping analysts understand whether a detected technique is part of a known campaign and what future steps might be anticipated.

By aligning threat detection with the phases of the kill chain, organizations gain strategic insight into attacker behavior and strengthen their ability to detect, contain, and disrupt threats before damage is done. Endpoint Detection and Response platforms are uniquely positioned to support this mapping through real-time visibility, historical telemetry, and automated correlation of events across systems. The threat lifecycle is a journey that adversaries undertake with specific goals in mind. Understanding that journey, phase by phase, is what allows defenders to stop them before they reach their destination. In the ever-changing battlefield of cybersecurity, kill chain mapping provides the structure and intelligence needed to navigate complexity and build a resilient defense.

Incident Response Playbooks for EDR

Incident response playbooks are structured, predefined sets of actions designed to guide security teams through the process of identifying, containing, eradicating, and recovering from cyber incidents. In the context of Endpoint Detection and Response, playbooks are essential for transforming alerts and telemetry into rapid, coordinated responses that minimize damage and restore normal operations. As EDR tools generate high volumes of data and potential alerts, playbooks help prioritize and streamline response efforts, ensuring that every stage of the incident lifecycle is addressed consistently and efficiently. They bridge the gap between detection and action, translating technical indicators into operational steps that can be executed by analysts, either manually or through automation.

A well-crafted incident response playbook starts with a clear definition of the incident type it addresses. Within an EDR framework, this could include malware infections, ransomware activity, credential theft, insider threats, unauthorized software installation, or lateral movement attempts. Each playbook must begin by outlining the conditions under which it should be triggered, which are usually tied to specific detection rules, indicators of compromise, or behavioral anomalies identified by the EDR system. The initial trigger is critical, as it ensures that the playbook is invoked only when the threat meets certain confidence thresholds, reducing the likelihood of false positives while ensuring prompt response to genuine threats.

Once an alert meets the criteria to activate a playbook, the next step is verification. EDR platforms often provide rich context around the alert, including process trees, file hashes, command-line arguments, registry changes, and network connections. The playbook should instruct analysts to review this data to confirm the legitimacy of the alert. This validation phase is important for filtering out benign anomalies and focusing attention on truly malicious activity. In advanced environments, this step can be partially or fully automated through machine learning models or integration with threat intelligence feeds that provide verdicts on observed artifacts.

After confirmation, containment becomes the immediate priority. The goal is to prevent the attacker from advancing further into the environment or causing additional harm. EDR systems provide several containment capabilities, including endpoint isolation, process termination, user session revocation, and blocking network communications. The playbook must outline which containment actions to take based on the nature and severity of the incident. For example, in the case of confirmed ransomware activity, full isolation of the endpoint is likely warranted. In contrast, for a suspicious login from an unusual location, it might be sufficient to suspend the user account and monitor associated endpoints for further activity.

Following containment, eradication focuses on removing the root cause of the incident. This involves deleting malicious files, uninstalling unauthorized applications, clearing persistence mechanisms, and patching exploited vulnerabilities. The playbook should specify exact remediation steps depending on the threat type. For malware infections, this might include restoring clean versions of affected files from backup. For credential-based attacks, it might require resetting passwords, rotating keys, and reviewing access logs. EDR tools assist in this process by identifying all components and processes associated with the threat, allowing analysts to ensure complete removal without leaving remnants that could lead to reinfection.

Recovery is the next critical phase and entails bringing affected systems back into normal operation. The playbook should guide teams on how to safely reintegrate isolated endpoints, validate system integrity, and ensure that no signs of compromise remain. It is essential to verify that endpoints are clean and that monitoring is in place to detect any recurrence of the threat. This stage often includes reimaging devices, restoring configurations, reapplying security baselines, and conducting post-recovery scans. Documentation of all recovery actions is important, both for auditing purposes and for future reference in case similar incidents arise.

Beyond the technical steps, incident response playbooks for EDR must include communication protocols. Security incidents often impact multiple stakeholders across the organization, including IT teams, legal departments, executive leadership, and potentially even customers or regulators. The playbook should identify roles and responsibilities, define internal and external communication plans, and provide templates for incident notifications. Clarity in communication is essential to maintain transparency, manage expectations, and meet regulatory reporting obligations, especially in incidents involving personal or sensitive data.

Each playbook should conclude with a post-incident review process. This includes collecting lessons learned, updating detection rules, refining the playbook itself, and sharing insights with the broader security team. EDR systems offer historical data that supports root cause analysis and helps teams understand how the attack occurred, what weaknesses were exploited, and how future incidents can be prevented. This feedback loop is a vital part of continuous improvement and ensures that the organization's defenses evolve alongside the threat landscape.

To maximize the effectiveness of EDR playbooks, organizations should integrate them with other tools in the security ecosystem. Integration with SIEM platforms allows alerts and actions to be correlated across systems, providing a holistic view of the incident. SOAR platforms can orchestrate the execution of playbooks, automate repetitive tasks, and escalate complex cases to human analysts. Ticketing systems can track playbook execution progress, assign responsibilities, and document resolution efforts. This interconnected environment reduces response times, eliminates gaps, and ensures that every incident is managed in a structured, accountable manner.

Developing effective playbooks requires collaboration across security, IT, compliance, and business units. Each group brings unique insights into the potential impact of incidents and the appropriate response strategies. Security teams must understand how IT operations can implement changes, IT must understand security priorities, and business leaders must understand risk. This collaboration ensures that playbooks are practical, effective, and aligned with organizational goals. Periodic testing through tabletop exercises or simulated attacks helps validate playbook accuracy, identify gaps, and ensure that team members are familiar with their roles.

As threats grow in sophistication and speed, the importance of having mature, actionable, and tested EDR playbooks cannot be overstated. They reduce reliance on individual expertise, ensure consistent response, and provide a framework for learning and adaptation. In a high-pressure environment where seconds matter, playbooks turn chaos into coordination and confusion into clarity. They are the operational bridge between detection and defense, enabling organizations to respond swiftly and decisively when every moment counts. By embedding playbooks into the core of their EDR strategy, organizations build not just a defense, but a disciplined, adaptive, and resilient approach to cyber incident response.

Data Privacy and EDR Logging

Endpoint Detection and Response platforms are critical tools for modern cybersecurity operations, offering unparalleled visibility into endpoint behavior and enabling organizations to detect, investigate, and respond to threats in real time. At the heart of their functionality is the collection and analysis of detailed telemetry from endpoints, including user activity, system processes, file interactions, and network communications. This depth of logging provides the forensic data needed to understand and respond to complex threats. However, as EDR platforms gather increasingly granular information, they also introduce new challenges related to data privacy. Organizations must carefully balance the need for security with the imperative to protect personal and sensitive information, particularly in an era of stringent privacy regulations and growing public concern over data usage and surveillance.

EDR logging includes a wide range of data types, many of which have privacy implications. These logs may capture usernames, login times, IP addresses, accessed files, opened applications, browsing history, and even typed commands or executed scripts. While this information is essential for detecting insider threats, identifying malicious behavior, and conducting forensic investigations, it can also reveal detailed patterns of user behavior, personal preferences, and work habits. In regulated industries or jurisdictions with strong privacy laws, such as those governed by the General Data Protection Regulation or the

California Consumer Privacy Act, collecting and processing this level of detail requires clear justification, transparency, and control.

One of the most pressing concerns related to EDR logging and data privacy is the potential for overcollection. Organizations may be tempted to collect as much data as possible under the assumption that more data equals better detection. However, indiscriminate data collection can violate privacy principles such as data minimization, which dictates that only data necessary for a specific purpose should be collected. To address this, EDR configurations must be carefully designed to capture only the telemetry required for security monitoring and incident response. This may involve disabling the collection of certain fields, anonymizing user data, or applying filters that exclude irrelevant or overly sensitive data points from being stored.

Another consideration is the retention of logged data. Privacy regulations often require organizations to limit the duration for which personal data is stored and to ensure that data is deleted when it is no longer necessary. EDR platforms typically allow administrators to configure retention periods for telemetry data, ensuring compliance with such requirements. These retention settings must align with the organization's security and compliance policies, as well as legal obligations. Retention periods should be long enough to support meaningful forensic investigations and compliance reporting, but not so long that they create unnecessary privacy risks or increase the potential impact of a data breach.

Access control is fundamental to maintaining privacy within EDR environments. Not all members of the security or IT teams need access to sensitive user data. Role-based access control mechanisms must be enforced to ensure that only authorized personnel can view or interact with personal information contained in logs. These controls should be complemented by audit trails that track who accessed what data and when, creating an accountability layer that discourages misuse and supports investigations into potential policy violations. Encryption of log data both at rest and in transit further protects sensitive information from unauthorized access, ensuring that even if data is intercepted or stolen, it remains unreadable.

Transparency is another key pillar of privacy in the context of EDR logging. Organizations must clearly communicate to employees and stakeholders what data is being collected, how it will be used, and what safeguards are in place to protect it. This transparency builds trust and ensures compliance with legal requirements that mandate notice and, in some cases, consent. Privacy policies and acceptable use agreements should reflect the use of EDR technologies, and employees should be educated about the types of data being monitored and their rights regarding that data. In some jurisdictions, employee consent may be required for certain types of monitoring, especially when it occurs outside of traditional work hours or involves personal devices.

The use of EDR in bring-your-own-device environments introduces additional privacy complexities. When personal devices are used to access corporate resources, EDR agents may inadvertently capture personal activity or data unrelated to work. To address this, organizations should implement segmentation strategies that separate corporate and personal data, ensuring that logging only occurs within the boundaries of corporate applications or secure containers. EDR solutions must support these technical boundaries and allow for flexible configurations that respect user privacy while maintaining security visibility.

Organizations must also consider the cross-border implications of EDR logging. In multinational companies, telemetry collected in one jurisdiction may be transmitted to servers located in another. This creates potential conflicts with data localization laws or cross-border data transfer restrictions. For example, some countries require that personal data be stored and processed within national borders unless specific safeguards or legal mechanisms are in place. EDR vendors and customers must collaborate to ensure that data storage, processing, and transmission practices are aligned with applicable laws and that data flows are protected by mechanisms such as standard contractual clauses or binding corporate rules.

Privacy impact assessments are a valuable tool for identifying and mitigating risks associated with EDR logging. These assessments evaluate the scope, necessity, and proportionality of data collection activities, as well as the technical and organizational measures in place to protect privacy. Conducting such assessments before deploying or updating EDR solutions helps organizations anticipate and address compliance challenges, demonstrate due diligence to regulators, and ensure that their use of security technology aligns with ethical standards and public expectations.

Finally, integrating privacy into the design of EDR tools and workflows—often referred to as privacy by design—is essential for long-term success. This involves embedding privacy considerations into every stage of the EDR lifecycle, from product selection and configuration to deployment and ongoing operations. Security and privacy should not be viewed as opposing forces but rather as complementary goals that can be achieved through thoughtful design, governance, and communication. By incorporating privacy principles into their EDR strategies, organizations can protect themselves from cyber threats while also respecting the rights and expectations of their users.

Data privacy and EDR logging are deeply intertwined aspects of cybersecurity practice. While EDR platforms provide the technical means to safeguard organizations from evolving threats, they must be implemented and operated in ways that uphold the principles of fairness, transparency, and accountability. In an age where trust is as valuable as technology, striking the right balance between visibility and privacy is not only a legal necessity but also a competitive advantage. When done correctly, EDR logging can support robust security without compromising the dignity or rights of individuals, allowing organizations to defend their environments with both precision and integrity.

Performance Impacts of EDR on Endpoints

Endpoint Detection and Response platforms have become a cornerstone of modern cybersecurity strategies, providing organizations with advanced capabilities to monitor, detect, investigate, and respond to threats originating on endpoint devices. While their security benefits are clear and substantial, EDR solutions can introduce performance impacts that affect endpoint responsiveness, user experience, and overall system efficiency. These performance concerns are not uniform across all deployments, as they depend on various factors such as endpoint hardware specifications, the scope of data collection, frequency of scans, the complexity of detection logic, and the extent of automated response actions. Nevertheless, understanding and managing the performance impact of EDR tools is essential to ensuring that security does not come at the cost of productivity or system stability.

One of the primary ways EDR affects endpoint performance is through continuous monitoring and telemetry collection. To deliver real-time visibility, EDR agents must observe and log activities such as process execution, file modifications, network connections, registry changes, and user behavior. This constant monitoring, especially when configured to capture high volumes of detailed data, requires CPU, memory, and disk resources. On lower-spec machines or devices already burdened with demanding applications, the additional resource consumption from the EDR agent can lead to noticeable slowdowns. Users may experience delayed application launches, lag during multitasking, or interruptions in workflows when system resources are strained by background monitoring tasks.

Scanning processes also contribute to performance impact. Many EDR solutions perform behavioral analysis or heuristic scanning in real time, evaluating each process or file against a set of known indicators or behavior models. These scans are essential for detecting threats such as fileless malware or zero-day exploits but can be resource-intensive if not carefully optimized. On-access scanning, in particular, where files are checked every time they are read, written, or executed, can increase I/O latency and reduce the performance of file-heavy operations. For example, development environments that compile large codebases, design workstations that render high-resolution media, or systems that frequently access large databases may see reduced efficiency due to constant scanning activity.

Memory usage is another important consideration. EDR agents reside in memory and must operate continuously in the background. Depending on the size of the telemetry cache, the number of active detection rules, and the sophistication of local analytics, the memory footprint of an agent can vary widely. On systems with limited RAM, such as older laptops or thin clients, the EDR agent may compete with essential applications for memory allocation, leading to swapping, degraded performance, or even application crashes. In some cases, multiple endpoint security agents from different vendors may be deployed simultaneously, compounding the issue and increasing the risk of resource contention.

Network performance can also be affected by EDR agents, especially those that upload telemetry or receive updates frequently. While many modern solutions are designed to transmit data efficiently, high-frequency uploads or large data bursts can strain bandwidth in environments with limited connectivity. This is particularly relevant in remote or branch offices, mobile users on metered networks, or environments relying on VPN tunnels. If telemetry transmission is not rate-limited or scheduled during off-peak hours, it may interfere with video calls, file transfers, or other business-critical network operations. Moreover, when EDR solutions rely on cloud-based analysis or sandboxing, the latency introduced by data round-trips to external servers can further affect the timeliness of detection and response.

Performance impacts are often magnified during peak EDR operations such as agent updates, full system scans, or threat containment actions. During these events, resource consumption spikes as the agent performs intensive operations like validating digital signatures, updating rule sets, scanning system memory, or executing response scripts. Without proper throttling or scheduling, these activities can disrupt users by consuming CPU cycles and locking system files. For instance, initiating a full scan during business hours can bring a workstation to a crawl, frustrating users and decreasing productivity. Similarly, containment actions that terminate processes or isolate devices from the network can disrupt legitimate tasks if executed without sufficient context or user notification.

Mitigating the performance impact of EDR involves both technical tuning and strategic planning. Most EDR platforms provide configuration options to optimize agent behavior for different endpoint roles. These settings may include adjusting the depth and frequency of scans, setting exclusions for known safe processes or directories, and controlling the timing of telemetry uploads. By tailoring the configuration to the specific use case of each endpoint— whether it is a developer workstation, an executive laptop, or a point-of-sale terminal—organizations can reduce unnecessary overhead and maintain a balance between visibility and performance.

Testing and piloting are critical steps in understanding the impact of EDR on endpoint performance. Before a wide-scale rollout, security teams should deploy the EDR agent in a controlled environment that includes various endpoint types and usage profiles. Monitoring system performance during typical workflows provides valuable data on how the agent behaves in real-world conditions. This testing phase allows teams to identify performance bottlenecks, adjust configurations, and validate compatibility with essential applications. It also helps build trust among end users by demonstrating that security controls are not being implemented at the expense of usability.

Collaboration between security teams, IT operations, and business units is essential when addressing EDR performance concerns. Security teams must communicate the value and necessity of EDR tools while being receptive to user feedback and operational realities. IT teams play a role in monitoring endpoint health, pushing updates, and ensuring that systems meet the minimum hardware requirements for smooth EDR operation. In some cases, hardware upgrades or system reallocation may be necessary to support advanced security capabilities without degrading user experience. Business units must be consulted to understand critical workflows and avoid disruptions during high-priority tasks.

EDR vendors also contribute to performance management by continuously refining their agents for efficiency. Advances in lightweight telemetry collection, incremental scanning, adaptive analytics, and intelligent scheduling help reduce the footprint of EDR solutions on endpoints. Cloud-native architectures that offload intensive analysis to cloud platforms rather than performing it locally further alleviate resource consumption. Organizations should regularly update EDR software to benefit from these improvements and work closely with vendors to troubleshoot any persistent issues that arise.

Ultimately, the performance impact of EDR on endpoints is a manageable challenge that must be addressed thoughtfully. It is the result of the trade-off between security and efficiency, a balance that can be achieved through customization, testing, and cross-functional cooperation. While no security solution is entirely free of overhead, the protection provided by EDR in detecting and containing sophisticated threats far outweighs its resource demands when deployed properly. Ensuring that endpoints remain responsive and reliable while being continuously monitored for threats is not just a technical objective but a strategic necessity for organizations that value both productivity and protection.

Managing EDR in Hybrid Environments

Managing Endpoint Detection and Response in hybrid environments presents unique challenges and opportunities that require a strategic blend of technology, policy, and operational coordination. A hybrid environment typically includes a mix of on-premises infrastructure, cloud-based services, remote workers, mobile devices, and virtualized platforms. As organizations transition to more flexible IT architectures to accommodate digital transformation, business agility, and remote workforces, the need for consistent and effective endpoint security across diverse environments becomes more pressing. EDR platforms are critical tools in this context because they provide visibility, detection, and response capabilities that span the full spectrum of endpoint types and locations. However, deploying and managing EDR effectively in such hybrid settings demands careful planning, robust architecture, and adaptive operational practices.

The first consideration in managing EDR across hybrid environments is establishing visibility across all endpoints, regardless of their physical or virtual location. Unlike traditional networks, where devices are mostly static and directly connected to the internal infrastructure, hybrid environments involve endpoints that operate across multiple domains, including corporate offices, home networks, public cloud platforms, and third-party service providers. EDR tools must be capable of maintaining continuous telemetry collection from all these endpoints, even when they are disconnected from the corporate VPN or operating in transient cloud workloads. This requires EDR agents that are lightweight, cloud-native, and resilient to varying network conditions. Ensuring uninterrupted visibility means that every endpoint, whether it's a physical laptop used by a traveling employee or a containerized application instance in a public cloud, remains within the scope of monitoring and control.

Centralized management becomes another foundational requirement. Hybrid environments often result in fragmented infrastructure managed by different teams, tools, and policies. An effective EDR solution must offer a centralized console through which security teams can monitor all endpoints, enforce policies, investigate alerts, and execute response actions. This centralized control plane must integrate seamlessly with identity and access management systems to authenticate users and assign role-based access to security data and actions. By using a single pane of glass, organizations can maintain consistent threat detection logic and response procedures, avoiding the pitfalls of disjointed or redundant toolsets. This also simplifies compliance reporting and audit readiness, which are particularly complex in environments where data resides across multiple jurisdictions and platforms.

Policy enforcement across hybrid endpoints poses significant challenges due to differences in operating systems, device types, and administrative domains. An endpoint policy that is appropriate for a managed Windows machine on a corporate network may not be suitable for a developer's MacBook accessing cloud repositories from a coffee shop. Therefore, EDR management must incorporate flexible policy frameworks that account for context, device posture, user role, and location. Conditional policy enforcement allows organizations to implement stronger controls on high-risk endpoints while enabling greater flexibility where appropriate. These dynamic policies ensure that security does not become a bottleneck to productivity, while still enforcing baseline protections that apply universally, such as malware prevention, behavioral anomaly detection, and alert generation for suspicious command-line activity.

Another critical element of EDR management in hybrid environments is the integration with other security and IT tools. In a distributed setting, information sharing between systems becomes essential for maintaining situational awareness and coordinating response efforts. EDR solutions must be able to feed telemetry into Security Information and Event Management platforms, contribute data to threat intelligence platforms, and trigger workflows in Security Orchestration, Automation, and Response solutions. Integration with cloud-native security tools is also important, particularly for monitoring virtual machines, containers, and serverless functions hosted in platforms such as AWS, Azure, or Google Cloud. These integrations provide context-rich threat visibility that spans beyond the endpoint and includes identity events, network flows, and application logs.

Remote and mobile workforce support is another major consideration. EDR agents must be capable of functioning independently of the corporate network and maintaining secure communication with the management console over the internet. This allows telemetry collection, alerting, and response to continue uninterrupted, even if the endpoint has not connected to the VPN in weeks. For organizations with a global presence, it is important that the EDR infrastructure includes geographically distributed cloud gateways or data collectors to ensure performance and reliability for endpoints connecting from different regions. Additionally, support for device mobility should extend to roaming policies that adapt based on location, such as applying stricter monitoring when the endpoint is on an untrusted network or outside of normal geofencing parameters.

Performance optimization is a recurring theme in hybrid EDR management. The diversity of endpoints in hybrid environments often means that resource constraints vary significantly across devices. Thin clients, virtual desktops, and mobile devices may not be able to support the same level of intensive scanning and analysis as fully resourced workstations. EDR platforms must therefore offer customizable deployment profiles and allow administrators to tune telemetry granularity, response automation, and scan frequencies based on endpoint role and capabilities. This ensures that EDR remains effective without degrading the performance of critical systems or frustrating users.

Incident response in hybrid environments also takes on added complexity. Investigating and responding to threats in a distributed landscape requires coordination across multiple teams, time zones, and administrative domains. EDR tools must support asynchronous investigations, collaborative workspaces, and real-time alerting to ensure that response actions are not delayed by organizational or geographic boundaries. Endpoint isolation, one of the most powerful containment tools, must be carefully implemented in hybrid settings to avoid disrupting critical workflows or leaving users stranded without access. Automated containment, quarantine, and remediation should be tested across all endpoint types to ensure that they perform reliably and safely in diverse conditions.

Compliance and regulatory requirements often introduce additional challenges when managing EDR in hybrid environments. Data residency laws, encryption mandates, and sector-specific controls must all be considered when selecting and configuring an EDR solution. The management platform must support secure storage, granular access control, and audit logging to satisfy these legal obligations. Moreover, organizations operating across international boundaries must ensure that endpoint telemetry is collected and processed in accordance with the data protection laws of each jurisdiction. Hybrid environments increase the likelihood that personal or sensitive data will traverse borders, making compliance a critical aspect of EDR strategy.

Finally, user awareness and training remain indispensable. In hybrid environments, where IT does not have direct control over every device or network, end users become frontline participants in the security process. EDR management must include efforts to educate users about what the tool does, what data is collected, how incidents are handled, and what to do when they receive a security notification. Building trust and transparency with users reduces friction, promotes cooperation, and improves incident reporting, which is often the first signal of a breach in remote or lightly monitored environments.

Managing EDR in hybrid environments is a continuous journey that requires adaptability, integration, and a deep understanding of the organization's evolving infrastructure. It is not merely a technical challenge but also an operational and cultural one. By deploying flexible tools, establishing centralized oversight, ensuring interoperability, and fostering user engagement, organizations can maintain strong endpoint security across complex, distributed environments while enabling the agility and innovation that hybrid architectures are designed to support.

Red and Blue Teaming with EDR Tools

Red and blue teaming are essential practices in modern cybersecurity operations, offering realistic simulations and defensive exercises that test and refine an organization's detection and response capabilities. Endpoint Detection and Response tools play a central role in these exercises, serving as both a target for offensive testing and a platform for defensive operations. The integration of EDR capabilities into red and blue team workflows elevates the quality of adversary emulation, enhances visibility into attack techniques, and strengthens an organization's ability to detect, investigate, and respond to advanced threats. The interplay between red and blue teams within the framework of EDR not only improves tactical readiness but also fosters a culture of continuous learning and resilience.

Red teaming involves the simulation of real-world adversaries by a group of offensive security experts who attempt to compromise systems using the same techniques, tactics, and procedures employed by actual attackers. Their goal is not merely to gain access but to test the limits of detection and response capabilities, identify weaknesses in defenses, and reveal blind spots in monitoring. Blue teaming, on the other hand, is the practice of defending against these simulated attacks in real time. Blue teams are tasked with identifying the threats, correlating evidence, launching investigations, and taking effective action to contain and mitigate the intrusion. EDR tools are the primary battleground for these engagements, providing the visibility, analytics, and response mechanisms that enable defenders to track and counter attacker movements.

From the red team's perspective, EDR tools represent both an obstacle and a challenge to be overcome. Effective red teams begin their engagements by conducting reconnaissance not only on network and system configurations but also on the security tools in place. If an EDR solution is known to be deployed, red teamers adjust their approach to avoid detection. This may include using living-off-the-land binaries, evading behavioral analytics, disabling or tampering with agents, and leveraging trusted processes to execute malicious payloads. The presence of a sophisticated EDR solution forces red teams to innovate and mimic the strategies of advanced persistent threat actors, thereby increasing the realism and value of the exercise.

EDR solutions record a wealth of endpoint telemetry, including process creation, command-line arguments, DLL loads, registry modifications, and network connections. Red teams seek to operate in ways that generate minimal or misleading telemetry, using stealthy techniques such as in-memory execution, process hollowing, or scheduled task abuse. They may attempt to blend in with normal system activity by launching attacks during business hours, using legitimate administrative tools like PowerShell or WMIC, and accessing systems through stolen credentials. These tactics create a challenging detection landscape for blue teams, who must sift through vast amounts of data to identify subtle deviations from expected behavior.

For blue teams, EDR platforms serve as the foundation of their defensive operations during red team exercises. Analysts rely on the EDR console to receive alerts, review process trees, analyze historical activity, and pivot across related data points. When a red team engages in credential dumping, for instance, the blue team may see suspicious access to LSASS memory, anomalous execution of Mimikatz-like commands, or the use of remote administrative tools without proper context. The challenge lies in connecting these indicators quickly and accurately, recognizing them as components of an active attack rather than isolated anomalies. EDR tools that provide intuitive visualizations, enriched context, and real-time search capabilities empower blue teams to act with greater speed and precision.

The effectiveness of EDR tools in red and blue teaming exercises depends heavily on the quality of detection rules and the maturity of response playbooks. Blue teams must maintain an up-to-date library of detection logic mapped to known adversary behaviors, often using frameworks like MITRE ATT&CK. Red team activity that aligns with specific tactics and techniques can trigger detections if those rules are in place. For example, attempts to establish persistence through registry run keys or scheduled tasks should be flagged by rules monitoring those activity paths. When detection occurs, automated or manual response playbooks guide the containment actions, such as isolating the endpoint, killing a process, or alerting the incident response team.

One of the key benefits of red and blue teaming with EDR is the ability to measure detection coverage and time-to-detect metrics under realistic conditions. EDR platforms that offer integrated detection mapping and telemetry playback enable teams to assess how quickly an attack was identified and how thoroughly it was understood. These metrics are essential for continuous improvement. They help identify where detection logic is missing, where false positives consume too much analyst time, and where response actions were delayed or ineffective. Over time, these exercises build institutional knowledge, validate technology investments, and ensure that security teams are prepared to face real-world adversaries.

Collaboration between red and blue teams is essential for maximizing the value of EDR-focused engagements. While the initial phases of a red team operation are conducted covertly to simulate real attack conditions, post-exercise debriefings allow both teams to compare notes, analyze gaps, and develop countermeasures. Red teams can share how they bypassed certain detections or exploited policy weaknesses, while blue teams can highlight where detections were successful and where deeper insight was needed. This feedback loop informs the refinement of EDR configurations, tuning of detection rules, development of new playbooks, and enhancement of user training.

EDR tools that support detailed logging, forensic data collection, and export capabilities further enrich this collaborative process. Logs from red team activities can be replayed in training environments, enabling blue teams to practice their investigative skills and test new detections. In advanced security operations centers, purple teaming exercises—where red and blue teams work together in real time—use EDR platforms as a shared foundation for experimentation, learning, and skill development. These collaborative models represent the next evolution of security readiness, where offensive and defensive expertise are combined to build a stronger overall posture.

As organizations mature in their use of EDR tools, red and blue teaming becomes less of a one-time exercise and more of a continuous, integrated function. Security teams conduct regular adversary simulations, threat hunting missions, and response drills, all grounded in the telemetry and capabilities provided by their EDR platforms. These activities not only prepare the organization for external threats but also foster a deeper understanding of internal systems, user behaviors, and operational risk. By embedding red and blue teaming into the lifecycle of EDR strategy, organizations gain a dynamic and adaptive defense capability, capable of evolving with the threat landscape and maintaining security resilience in the face of sophisticated adversaries.

EDR Reporting and Executive Dashboards

Endpoint Detection and Response solutions generate a tremendous volume of data that can be analyzed, visualized, and communicated through robust reporting mechanisms and executive dashboards. These tools are essential not only for operational security teams but also for executive stakeholders who need to understand the organization's threat landscape, risk posture, and incident response capabilities at a glance. EDR reporting and dashboards act as a bridge between technical depth and strategic oversight, transforming raw telemetry into meaningful insights that support decision-making, policy development, and resource allocation. The effectiveness of an EDR implementation is often judged not just by its detection power but by its ability to communicate its value clearly and consistently to different audiences across the organization.

One of the primary goals of EDR reporting is to provide visibility into the security status of the endpoint fleet. Reports typically include metrics on the number and type of alerts generated, endpoints monitored, threat detections, response actions taken, and coverage against specific tactics or techniques. These metrics help operational teams track the effectiveness of their detection rules, monitor alert volumes for signs of unusual activity, and assess whether response workflows are functioning as intended. For example, if the number of high-severity alerts spikes over a short period, it may indicate the emergence of a new attack campaign or the exploitation of a previously unknown vulnerability. Such trends allow teams to prioritize investigation and adapt their strategies in real time.

Executive dashboards, by contrast, are designed for high-level consumption. They focus less on individual alerts and more on aggregated data that reflects broader patterns and trends. An effective executive dashboard presents concise summaries of critical information such as top threats observed, most targeted assets, incident response time, endpoint compliance status, and detection coverage against industry frameworks like MITRE ATT&CK. These dashboards serve to answer key business questions: Are we improving our response capabilities? Are we detecting advanced threats before they cause damage? Are our investments in EDR yielding measurable improvements in security posture? By translating technical activity into business impact, executive dashboards help bridge the gap between cybersecurity and business leadership.

Customization is a critical feature in both reporting and dashboards. Different stakeholders have different informational needs, and EDR platforms must offer flexible templates and dynamic filtering to accommodate them. A security operations center may require detailed reports on every endpoint flagged for suspicious behavior in the past 24 hours, including process trees and associated indicators of compromise. Meanwhile, a CISO may prefer a weekly summary that tracks trends over time, such as average time to detect, time to respond, and the ratio of true positives to false positives. Granular filtering capabilities allow reports to be tailored by geography, business unit, endpoint type, or user role, enabling more targeted and actionable insights.

Visualizations play an essential role in making EDR data understandable and impactful. Charts, heatmaps, timelines, and trend lines can communicate complex patterns more effectively than raw data tables. A line graph showing the decline in mean time to respond over several months tells a story of operational improvement. A pie chart breaking down alerts by severity helps prioritize resource allocation. A heatmap of attack techniques observed across departments may reveal gaps in employee training or endpoint hardening. Visual elements allow both technical and non-technical audiences to grasp the implications of the data quickly and intuitively, increasing the overall value of the EDR reporting ecosystem.

Automated reporting is another cornerstone of effective EDR communication. Reports that are generated and distributed on a regular schedule ensure that stakeholders remain informed without placing a constant burden on security analysts. Whether sent daily, weekly, or monthly, these automated reports help establish a rhythm of security awareness and accountability across the organization. They can be delivered in various formats, such as PDFs for executive consumption, CSVs for data analysis, or interactive web-based dashboards for real-time exploration. Integrations with email platforms, collaboration tools, and ticketing systems further enhance the accessibility and relevance of EDR reports.

Compliance and audit readiness are additional dimensions where EDR reporting proves indispensable. Many regulatory frameworks require organizations to maintain detailed records of security events, access controls, response actions, and endpoint configurations. EDR platforms can be configured to generate compliance-specific reports that document how threats were handled, what evidence was collected, and whether policy violations occurred. These reports serve as documentation for auditors, regulators, and legal teams, ensuring that the organization can demonstrate due diligence and adherence to industry standards. In some cases, real-time dashboards can be shared with compliance teams to provide ongoing assurance rather than relying solely on periodic audits.

Incident-specific reporting is also crucial during and after security events. When an incident occurs, stakeholders need to understand what happened, how it was detected, what actions were taken, and what the impact was. EDR platforms support this by allowing analysts to compile incident timelines, affected endpoints, user activity, and forensic artifacts into a comprehensive report. These reports can be used to inform internal reviews, refine playbooks, and communicate findings to external stakeholders if necessary. In post-incident reviews, such reporting helps organizations evaluate their response effectiveness and uncover areas for improvement.

Reporting is also essential for long-term strategic planning. By analyzing trends over time, organizations can identify recurring threat vectors, vulnerable asset types, and detection blind spots. These insights inform decisions about future investments in technology, training, and process refinement. For example, if reports consistently show that credential theft techniques are prevalent and frequently successful, it may prompt investment in stronger identity and access management solutions or user awareness training. Conversely, if EDR data reveals that certain types of alerts are rarely investigated or resolved, it may indicate a need for automation, staffing adjustments, or rule optimization.

The ability of an EDR solution to support robust reporting and executive dashboards is not just a convenience; it is a critical feature that defines its operational maturity. Security is no longer a purely technical function—it is a strategic pillar of business continuity, brand protection, and customer trust. For this reason, the ability to communicate clearly about threat landscapes, response effectiveness, and risk trends is indispensable. EDR tools that fail to offer meaningful reporting capabilities leave organizations flying blind, unable to articulate their security posture to those responsible for governance and oversight.

As the threat landscape continues to evolve, EDR reporting and executive dashboards will play an increasingly important role in shaping proactive defense strategies. They provide the data needed to justify budgets, guide policies, and prioritize action. They transform complex technical signals into coherent narratives of resilience and risk management. And perhaps most importantly, they ensure that cybersecurity remains visible, measurable, and aligned with the strategic objectives of the organization. In a world where threats move fast and decisions must be data-driven, EDR reporting is not an afterthought—it is the foundation of informed, agile, and accountable security leadership.

Adversary Emulation and Testing EDR

Adversary emulation is a critical practice in the continuous validation of security tools, processes, and personnel, particularly within the framework of Endpoint Detection and Response solutions. It involves simulating the behavior of real-world threat actors in a controlled environment to evaluate how effectively detection and response mechanisms perform. Unlike traditional penetration testing, which focuses on identifying and exploiting vulnerabilities, adversary emulation is designed to mimic the tactics, techniques, and procedures of specific threat groups as documented in threat intelligence frameworks such as MITRE ATT&CK. This approach allows security teams to test not only the technical capabilities of their EDR platform but also the readiness of their analysts, the accuracy of detection logic, and the efficiency of their incident response playbooks. By proactively challenging their defenses, organizations can find gaps before adversaries do, refine their detection strategies, and ensure that their EDR solutions are functioning as intended under realistic conditions.

An effective adversary emulation campaign begins with threat modeling. Security teams select a threat actor that is relevant to their industry, geography, or infrastructure, often based on current threat intelligence or historical attack data. Each threat actor typically employs a well-documented set of techniques, ranging from phishing and credential harvesting to lateral movement, data exfiltration, and persistence. By selecting a known adversary and mapping their behaviors to the enterprise environment, the emulation becomes contextualized and meaningful. The objective is not merely to generate alerts, but to understand whether the EDR solution is capable of detecting and responding to the actual techniques that would be used by a threat actor targeting the organization.

Once the threat model is defined, emulation scripts and tools are prepared to simulate each stage of the attack. These tools may include open-source frameworks like Atomic Red Team, Caldera, or commercial platforms specifically designed for adversary simulation. The scenarios include step-by-step implementations of behaviors such as privilege escalation using token manipulation, credential access through LSASS memory scraping, execution of payloads via PowerShell or WMI, and persistence through registry run keys or scheduled tasks.

Each step is executed with careful monitoring to observe how the EDR platform logs the activity, whether it generates alerts, and how it correlates with other telemetry. Analysts track which behaviors are detected, which are missed, and how quickly alerts are generated and triaged.

During emulation, it is essential to measure not only the raw detection rate but also the quality of context provided by the EDR platform. A high-fidelity detection includes not just an alert, but also rich metadata such as the parent and child process relationships, command-line arguments, file hashes, user context, and network connections. This contextual data is crucial for analysts attempting to understand the full scope of the attack and make informed response decisions. For instance, detecting the execution of a suspicious script is helpful, but understanding that it was launched by a trusted process during a time window when the user was not logged in adds a layer of investigative depth that can shift an alert from informational to actionable.

Adversary emulation is also a powerful way to test the responsiveness of automated or manual playbooks within the EDR platform. When malicious behavior is detected, organizations expect their EDR tools to initiate predefined response actions such as isolating the endpoint, terminating malicious processes, quarantining suspicious files, or alerting key personnel. Emulation allows teams to validate whether these actions are triggered correctly, whether they are executed promptly, and whether they cause any unintended consequences. For example, if an endpoint is isolated due to a false positive, it may disrupt critical business operations. Testing these scenarios in advance allows for the refinement of thresholds, playbook logic, and escalation procedures to minimize such risks.

Collaboration between offensive and defensive teams enhances the value of adversary emulation. Red teams or third-party testers executing the emulation provide insight into how closely their activity mirrored real attacker behavior and what evasion techniques were successful. Blue teams, operating the EDR solution, contribute observations about detection gaps, delayed alerts, or unexpected blind spots. This exchange of knowledge creates a feedback loop where each round of testing improves the organization's ability to detect and respond to real threats. These exercises also help prioritize detection engineering efforts, ensuring that security resources are directed toward closing the most critical gaps.

Another benefit of adversary emulation is its role in improving the training and readiness of security analysts. When analysts are exposed to realistic attack scenarios in a controlled setting, they develop the investigative skills and intuition needed to respond effectively during actual incidents. The repetition of observing, triaging, and responding to simulated threats builds muscle memory, reduces response times, and fosters a deeper understanding of how adversaries operate. EDR platforms that allow historical search and replay capabilities can extend this training by enabling analysts to review past emulation data, explore alternate investigative paths, and compare outcomes.

Adversary emulation also contributes to long-term security strategy by providing metrics and evidence for leadership and governance. Reports generated from these exercises can quantify detection coverage, highlight improvements over time, and justify investments in additional tooling, personnel, or training. By aligning emulation results with threat intelligence and business risk, security leaders can communicate the value of their EDR deployment in tangible terms. These insights also support compliance and audit requirements by demonstrating that the organization is actively testing and validating its defensive controls against known threats.

In cloud and hybrid environments, adversary emulation must be adapted to test EDR coverage beyond traditional endpoints. Simulating attacks on virtual machines, containers, or cloud workloads requires emulation tools that understand the unique execution environments and telemetry formats of these platforms. EDR solutions must be tested not only for their ability to detect behaviors in cloud-hosted systems but also for their ability to maintain consistent visibility and control across disparate infrastructure. As organizations increasingly adopt cloud-native technologies, the scope of adversary emulation must evolve accordingly, ensuring that all assets remain protected.

The ultimate goal of adversary emulation in the context of EDR is to move from reactive detection to proactive resilience. Rather than waiting for a real attacker to test the limits of security controls, organizations take the initiative to challenge themselves, learn from failures, and iterate continuously. By simulating real-world threats and measuring the effectiveness of detection, response, and investigation processes, security teams transform their EDR platforms from passive data collectors into active engines of security validation and improvement. This discipline not only sharpens technical defenses but also builds the confidence, agility, and institutional knowledge required to defend against the constantly evolving tactics of modern cyber adversaries.

Selecting the Right EDR Vendor

Selecting the right Endpoint Detection and Response vendor is one of the most critical decisions a security team can make, as it directly impacts an organization's ability to detect, analyze, and respond to threats across its endpoint infrastructure. The EDR solution serves as both the frontline and the last line of defense, monitoring endpoints in real time, identifying malicious activity, and providing the tools necessary for containment and investigation. With the growing sophistication of cyber threats and the increasing complexity of IT environments, the selection of an EDR vendor must be based on a comprehensive understanding of both technical and operational requirements, as well as the vendor's ability to align with an organization's long-term security strategy. It is not a matter of simply choosing the most popular or well-marketed product, but of identifying a solution that fits seamlessly into the organization's unique ecosystem while offering flexibility, scalability, and reliability under real-world conditions.

One of the first steps in selecting an EDR vendor is identifying the specific needs of the organization. These needs are shaped by multiple factors including industry regulations, existing infrastructure, operational maturity, available personnel, and the threat landscape relevant to the business. A healthcare organization will have different priorities than a financial institution, just as a multinational enterprise will differ in scope and complexity from a mid-sized manufacturing company. Understanding these unique factors allows security leaders to create a list of required capabilities, such as support for hybrid environments, integration with identity and access management tools, or compliance with data residency laws. This list becomes the foundation for evaluating EDR vendors not just on features, but on their ability to solve real problems in context.

Detection capability is often the most scrutinized aspect of EDR solutions, and rightly so. The core function of any EDR platform is to accurately identify suspicious or malicious activity on endpoints without generating excessive false positives. Prospective vendors should be evaluated based on their detection techniques, which can include signature-based detection, behavioral analysis, heuristic modeling, and machine learning algorithms. An ideal EDR solution will combine these techniques to cover a broad range of attack vectors while minimizing noise. Buyers should request detailed information about how detections are generated and validated, and whether the solution provides transparency into the logic behind its alerts. The ability to map detections to frameworks such as MITRE ATT&CK is also a strong indicator of maturity and operational alignment.

Equally important as detection is the platform's response functionality. A strong EDR vendor offers robust response tools such as remote process termination, file quarantine, device isolation, and live terminal access for deeper forensic investigation. These features must be accessible through a streamlined interface that allows analysts to act swiftly during an incident. Additionally, automation and orchestration capabilities are increasingly critical, especially for teams that must handle large volumes of alerts or operate with limited resources. Vendors that offer customizable playbooks and integrations with SOAR platforms enable more efficient and consistent incident response. The response capabilities of the EDR platform should be tested in real-world scenarios or simulated attacks to assess their reliability, speed, and potential impact on system performance.

Scalability and performance are essential technical considerations, particularly for organizations with a large and diverse endpoint fleet. The EDR agent must operate efficiently across different operating systems, hardware configurations, and connectivity scenarios. It should collect and transmit telemetry without overloading system resources or network bandwidth. Moreover, the backend infrastructure—whether cloud-based or on-premises—must be capable of ingesting, storing, and processing data at scale without introducing delays in detection or analysis. Prospective vendors should provide benchmarks, reference architectures, and customer case studies that demonstrate their solution's performance under similar workloads and deployment conditions.

Integration is another major factor in vendor selection. No EDR solution exists in isolation; it must interoperate with other components of the organization's security stack, including SIEMs, identity providers, threat intelligence platforms, vulnerability management tools, and more. The ability to share data, trigger actions, and correlate events across systems significantly enhances the overall value of the EDR platform. Vendors should support open APIs, prebuilt connectors, and robust documentation to facilitate integration. Compatibility with existing workflows and technologies not only accelerates deployment but also reduces friction in day-to-day operations, allowing security teams to maximize their investment.

Vendor support and partnership quality can also be deciding factors. Organizations should evaluate the responsiveness, expertise, and availability of the vendor's support teams. This includes assessing the quality of onboarding and training programs, the availability of technical documentation and community forums, and the frequency and transparency of software updates. A strong vendor partnership goes beyond just providing a product—it involves active collaboration, threat sharing, and strategic alignment to help the customer continuously improve their security posture. Prospective customers should engage in reference calls, participate in trials, and review service level agreements to gain confidence in the vendor's commitment to long-term success.

Cost is always a consideration, but it should be approached holistically. The total cost of ownership includes not only the licensing fees but also the costs associated with deployment, management, training, and potential impact on IT operations. An EDR solution that appears affordable upfront may become expensive if it requires significant customization, generates excessive false positives, or lacks critical capabilities that must be compensated with additional tools. A well-chosen EDR platform should reduce risk, improve efficiency, and consolidate multiple functions, thereby generating value that exceeds its cost. A careful financial analysis should consider both direct and indirect benefits, as well as the potential cost of a security breach mitigated by timely detection and response.

Security teams should also consider the vendor's innovation roadmap and alignment with emerging threats. The cybersecurity landscape evolves rapidly, and an EDR solution that is effective today must be continuously improved to remain effective tomorrow. Vendors that invest in research and development, participate in public security initiatives, and respond quickly to new attack techniques demonstrate the agility required in modern threat environments. Prospective buyers should ask about planned features, product development cycles, and the vendor's vision for the future of endpoint security.

Selecting the right EDR vendor is a complex but vital process that requires deep engagement from technical, operational, and strategic stakeholders. It involves balancing technical excellence with practical usability, short-term needs with long-term goals, and cost considerations with security outcomes. When done thoroughly, this process results in more than just the acquisition of a tool—it leads to the establishment of a foundational pillar of the organization's security posture. An EDR solution that aligns with the organization's objectives, integrates seamlessly into its environment, and evolves alongside its threats becomes not just a product, but a trusted partner in the ongoing mission to protect assets, users, and data in an increasingly hostile digital world.

Cost-Benefit Analysis of EDR Investments

Investing in Endpoint Detection and Response solutions is increasingly seen as a necessary strategy for organizations seeking to strengthen their cybersecurity posture and reduce the risks associated with advanced threats. While the value of EDR solutions is often discussed in technical terms such as improved detection capabilities or faster incident response, decision-makers must also assess their impact through the lens of financial and operational return on investment. A thorough cost-benefit analysis of EDR investments helps organizations determine whether the deployment of such technologies aligns with their broader business objectives and provides measurable value over time. This evaluation is particularly relevant in a climate where cybersecurity budgets must be justified and allocated effectively across a range of competing priorities.

The initial costs associated with implementing an EDR solution typically include licensing fees, infrastructure upgrades, deployment services, and training for personnel. Licensing models may vary from one vendor to another, with some charging per endpoint, while others offer tiered pricing based on feature sets or organizational size. Infrastructure costs may be incurred if the chosen EDR platform requires on-premises servers or hybrid configurations, although many modern EDR solutions are cloud-native and reduce the need for internal infrastructure investment. Deployment services, including professional services for integration and configuration, can also contribute to upfront expenditures, especially in large or complex environments. Finally, the human element is significant, as staff must be trained not only in using the EDR console but also in interpreting alerts, conducting investigations, and executing response playbooks.

In addition to these initial costs, organizations must account for ongoing operational expenses. These include annual license renewals, support and maintenance fees, and the personnel costs associated with managing and responding to EDR-generated alerts. Depending on the alert volume and detection logic, an EDR platform can generate a high number of events requiring triage. If the system is not properly tuned, this can lead to alert fatigue and resource drain. Organizations may also need to invest in additional security analysts or leverage managed detection and response services to ensure timely and accurate threat response. While these ongoing expenses are necessary for maintaining a strong security posture, they must be evaluated in relation to the operational capacity and maturity of the security team.

The benefits of EDR investments, while sometimes less tangible, are often more significant than the costs when evaluated over the medium to long term. One of the primary benefits is the reduction in risk exposure. By providing real-time visibility into endpoint activity and enabling rapid containment of threats, EDR solutions help prevent data breaches, ransomware outbreaks, and operational disruptions. The financial impact of a major breach can be catastrophic, including regulatory fines, legal expenses, customer churn, and reputational damage. EDR helps mitigate these risks by detecting early-stage compromise, preventing lateral movement, and supporting root cause analysis to prevent recurrence. The cost avoidance associated with preventing even a single successful breach can easily outweigh the annual cost of maintaining an EDR platform.

Another key benefit is the improved efficiency of the security operations team. EDR platforms streamline detection and response workflows by centralizing telemetry, enriching alerts with context, and automating repetitive tasks. This enables analysts to focus on high-priority incidents and respond more quickly and effectively. Faster response times mean shorter dwell times for attackers, reducing the potential damage they can inflict. Improved analyst efficiency can also defer or eliminate the need to hire additional personnel, representing a substantial operational savings over time. Additionally, when paired with automation and orchestration tools, EDR platforms can execute response actions such as device isolation, process termination, or file quarantine without human intervention, further increasing the return on investment.

The value of EDR solutions extends beyond threat detection and response. They also support compliance, audit readiness, and cyber insurance requirements. Many regulatory frameworks require organizations to demonstrate the ability to detect and respond to security incidents. EDR solutions provide the logging, reporting, and investigative capabilities needed to meet these requirements. This reduces the risk of non-compliance and associated fines while also simplifying the audit process. For organizations seeking or maintaining cyber insurance coverage, demonstrating the presence of EDR controls can result in more favorable policy terms, including lower premiums and higher coverage limits. These financial incentives directly contribute to the return on EDR investments.

Quantifying the value of EDR also involves examining the improvement in security metrics over time. Organizations can track key performance indicators such as mean time to detect, mean time to respond, the number of incidents contained, the percentage of endpoints monitored, and the reduction in false positives. These metrics not only demonstrate the operational effectiveness of the EDR platform but also provide evidence of increased security maturity.

When security leaders can show consistent improvement in these areas, it reinforces the case for continued investment in the platform and related technologies. It also builds trust with executive stakeholders and board members who require evidence of cybersecurity efficacy and fiscal responsibility.

In the context of strategic planning, EDR investments can also enable future cost savings through tool consolidation. Many EDR platforms include capabilities that overlap with other endpoint security tools, such as antivirus, host-based intrusion detection systems, or application control. By replacing multiple point solutions with a single, integrated platform, organizations can reduce licensing costs, simplify management, and decrease the likelihood of configuration conflicts. This consolidation also reduces the complexity of security architecture, making it easier to maintain and less prone to human error.

Beyond the purely financial aspects, there are intangible but important benefits to EDR investments. These include increased confidence among customers and partners, enhanced brand reputation, and greater internal alignment around cybersecurity objectives. A visible and effective EDR deployment signals that the organization takes security seriously, which can be a competitive differentiator in industries where trust and reliability are paramount. Employees, too, benefit from the peace of mind that comes from knowing their systems and data are being actively monitored and protected.

Ultimately, the cost-benefit analysis of EDR investments must be framed within the broader context of organizational risk management and resilience. While the upfront and operational costs may seem high, the value delivered in terms of risk reduction, operational efficiency, compliance readiness, and strategic enablement makes EDR a sound and often essential investment. The most successful organizations are those that do not view EDR as a reactive expense but as a proactive enabler of business continuity, competitive advantage, and long-term digital trust. By applying a rigorous and forward-looking cost-benefit analysis, security leaders can build a compelling case for EDR that resonates with both technical and executive stakeholders, ensuring sustained support and strategic alignment across the enterprise.

Integration with Endpoint Configuration Management

Integrating Endpoint Detection and Response solutions with endpoint configuration management systems creates a powerful synergy that enhances visibility, streamlines policy enforcement, and improves the efficiency of both security and IT operations. Endpoint configuration management involves the centralized control of device settings, software installations, user permissions, patch levels, and compliance baselines across the entire endpoint environment. It ensures that endpoints adhere to the organization's operational standards and security policies. When combined with the deep behavioral telemetry and forensic capabilities of an EDR platform, this integration enables a more holistic, proactive, and responsive approach to endpoint security and health management. In modern, distributed enterprise environments, where devices span multiple operating systems, geographies, and usage patterns, this integration is not just beneficial—it is essential.

The foundation of this integration lies in unifying visibility across both system configuration data and real-time endpoint behavior. Configuration management systems can report on the status of antivirus software, firewall settings, patch levels, encryption status, and installed applications. EDR platforms, meanwhile, provide insight into how those applications are used, what processes are executed, how the network stack behaves, and whether suspicious activities are occurring. Together, these data sets give administrators a complete view of an endpoint's posture, allowing them to cross-reference misconfigurations or compliance deviations with observed risk indicators. For example, if a configuration tool reports that a device is missing a critical security patch and the EDR platform simultaneously detects unusual command-line activity on that system, security teams can rapidly escalate the issue and prioritize remediation.

Another key benefit of integration is policy alignment and enforcement. Configuration management tools typically deploy security baselines that define the desired state of endpoints, including allowed services, password policies, logging settings, and access controls. When endpoints drift from this desired state, alerts are generated, and corrective actions can be taken. However, traditional configuration management platforms often lack the ability to detect adversarial manipulation or the execution of unauthorized scripts in real time. EDR platforms fill this gap by offering behavioral detection and response capabilities that can immediately identify when an attacker attempts to bypass or disable configured controls. By integrating the two systems, organizations can enforce configuration policies with the confidence that EDR will catch any real-time attempts to undermine them, creating a dual layer of defense.

This integration also improves the accuracy and speed of incident triage and remediation. When an alert is generated by the EDR system, analysts need context to determine its severity and the best course of action. Having immediate access to configuration data about the affected device, such as its user group, installed software, patch history, and baseline status, enables analysts to make informed decisions faster. Conversely, when configuration tools detect unauthorized changes to a device, such as the installation of unapproved software or modifications to system registries, they can trigger a cross-platform investigation within the EDR console to determine whether those changes correlate with known attack behaviors. This bidirectional flow of information allows for smarter alert correlation and reduces both false positives and missed detections.

Automation is another area where integration delivers substantial value. Configuration management platforms often support scripted actions or workflows that can be triggered in response to policy violations. EDR platforms offer similar automation for threat response, such as quarantining a file or isolating a device from the network. When these systems are integrated, security teams can orchestrate complex, cross-system responses that combine the strengths of both. For example, if an EDR alert identifies a device exhibiting signs of ransomware activity, the response could involve isolating the endpoint using EDR, reverting its configuration to a known good state using the configuration tool, and then triggering a patch compliance check to ensure all recent vulnerabilities have been addressed. This level of coordination reduces response times, limits damage, and restores operational integrity without manual intervention.

Scalability and operational efficiency are also enhanced by this integration. Managing thousands or even tens of thousands of endpoints manually is impractical. Configuration management tools already provide the infrastructure to group devices, apply changes at scale, and monitor compliance over time. By incorporating EDR telemetry into these workflows, organizations can not only enforce baseline configurations but also validate their effectiveness in reducing risk. Devices can be grouped not just by operating system or function, but also by behavioral risk indicators observed by the EDR platform. High-risk groups may receive stricter configuration policies, additional monitoring, or prioritized updates. This dynamic approach to policy enforcement ensures that the organization's security posture adapts in real time based on actual threat conditions, rather than static assumptions.

Reporting and compliance readiness are also improved. Both EDR and configuration management platforms generate logs and reports used to demonstrate regulatory compliance and support audits. By integrating the two, organizations can produce unified reports that show not only that configuration standards were applied but also that they were effective in preventing or containing security incidents. These reports can detail the lifecycle of a threat, from initial detection to endpoint remediation and policy restoration, providing a complete narrative that satisfies both technical reviewers and regulatory bodies. In sectors such as finance, healthcare, or government, where accountability is paramount, this level of transparency is invaluable.

The integration of EDR and configuration management systems also supports proactive risk management. Configuration management data can be used to identify endpoints that are especially vulnerable, such as those running outdated operating systems, lacking encryption, or deviating from patch baselines. These endpoints can be flagged within the EDR platform for heightened monitoring or subjected to additional detection rules. Similarly, EDR behavior data can reveal endpoints that, while appearing compliant from a configuration perspective, are acting suspiciously or engaging in unusual network activity. This bidirectional analysis helps security teams shift from reactive firefighting to proactive risk identification and mitigation.

From a strategic perspective, the integration of EDR and endpoint configuration management reinforces the principle of defense in depth. While each solution independently addresses critical components of endpoint security, their combined use creates overlapping layers of control that enhance resilience. Configuration management ensures that devices start in a known secure state and remain compliant over time, while EDR ensures that any deviation from that state is detected and addressed swiftly. Together, they offer a comprehensive solution for managing the complexity, dynamism, and threat exposure of modern endpoint environments.

For organizations seeking to maximize the value of their EDR investment, integration with endpoint configuration management systems is no longer optional. It is a force multiplier that enhances visibility, reduces response times, ensures compliance, and ultimately strengthens the entire security framework. As threats become more sophisticated and regulatory demands more stringent, this integration provides a path forward to a more intelligent, automated, and adaptive approach to endpoint defense. By aligning technical capabilities with operational goals and strategic outcomes, security teams can ensure that their defenses are not only reactive but also resilient, coordinated, and continuously improving.

Addressing Insider Threats with EDR

Insider threats represent one of the most complex and potentially damaging categories of cybersecurity risk. Unlike external attackers who must find a way into a network, insiders already have legitimate access to systems and data. They may be employees, contractors, or third-party partners who either intentionally or unintentionally cause harm. These threats can involve malicious actions such as data theft, sabotage, or espionage, as well as negligent behaviors like mishandling sensitive information or falling victim to social engineering. Because insiders operate within the boundaries of authorized access, their activities are often difficult to detect using traditional security measures. Endpoint Detection and Response platforms offer a unique advantage in addressing insider threats by providing deep, continuous visibility into user behavior and system activity, enabling real-time detection of suspicious actions and supporting rapid, targeted responses.

One of the core strengths of EDR in the context of insider threat detection is its ability to collect and analyze granular endpoint telemetry. This includes process execution, file access, registry modifications, network connections, and user interactions. By continuously monitoring these data points, EDR tools create a behavioral baseline for each user and device. Any deviations from this baseline can be flagged as anomalies for further investigation. For example, if a user who normally works with HR documents suddenly starts accessing customer databases or transferring large amounts of data to an external drive, the EDR system can generate an alert for potential data exfiltration. This level of behavioral analysis allows organizations to spot threats that might otherwise go unnoticed.

Insider threats can be particularly challenging because they do not always involve overtly malicious tools or techniques. A disgruntled employee may use legitimate applications and credentials to access sensitive data, making their actions indistinguishable from routine work on the surface. EDR tools help bridge this gap by correlating multiple behaviors across time and context. If a user accesses sensitive files outside of normal working hours, uses remote desktop connections inappropriately, or attempts to disable endpoint security features, these activities can be pieced together by the EDR platform to identify a potential threat. The ability to trace sequences of actions and reconstruct timelines is critical for uncovering the subtle patterns that indicate insider misuse.

Response capabilities are equally important when dealing with insider threats. Once suspicious behavior is detected, the organization must act quickly to contain the threat without causing unnecessary disruption. EDR platforms enable a range of response actions, such as isolating the endpoint from the network, terminating unauthorized processes, revoking user credentials, and logging the user out of all systems. These actions can be executed remotely and with precision, limiting the insider's ability to continue their activities while preserving evidence for investigation. In cases where intent is unclear or additional validation is needed, EDR tools allow security teams to monitor the endpoint more closely without alerting the user, enabling a covert investigation to confirm or refute suspicions.

Insider threats also often involve data movement, whether it be copying files to external media, sending them via email, or uploading them to cloud services. EDR platforms monitor these channels and can detect behaviors such as file compression, encryption before transfer, or unusual data volumes being moved. For example, an employee preparing to leave the company might start compiling proprietary information into zip files or send large email attachments to their personal account. These actions, especially when correlated with HR events like resignation notices, can provide early warning signs of potential data theft. Alerts can be configured to trigger automated workflows that notify security teams, initiate endpoint surveillance, or escalate to legal or compliance departments.

Visibility into user behavior is essential for distinguishing between malicious intent and accidental mistakes. Not all insider threats stem from malice; many are the result of ignorance, carelessness, or confusion. An employee might accidentally email a confidential document to the wrong recipient or fall for a phishing attempt that grants external actors internal access. EDR tools provide context to these incidents by showing the full sequence of events. Was the file accessed for the first time just before it was sent? Were any macros enabled in the email attachment? Did the user's device begin communicating with suspicious IP addresses afterward? This context allows organizations to tailor their responses appropriately, whether that means launching a full investigation or providing user training and awareness.

A robust insider threat program supported by EDR also includes proactive threat hunting. Security teams can use EDR search capabilities to look for behaviors indicative of insider misuse, even in the absence of alerts. Queries might target the use of administrative tools by non-administrative users, the execution of scripts from unauthorized directories, or the presence of uncommon browser extensions. Regular hunting exercises help uncover dormant threats and improve the organization's overall readiness. These efforts are further enhanced when EDR platforms integrate with identity and access management systems, allowing hunters to correlate endpoint activity with user identities, roles, and access privileges.

Policy enforcement is another critical aspect of insider threat management that benefits from EDR integration. Organizations may have strict policies around which users can access sensitive data, use USB devices, or install software. EDR tools can monitor for policy violations in real time and enforce restrictions automatically. If a user attempts to disable endpoint protection, plug in an unauthorized device, or run a banned application, the EDR system can block the action and alert security personnel. These preventive controls not only reduce the risk of insider abuse but also demonstrate the organization's commitment to strong data governance and accountability.

EDR platforms also support incident investigation and forensic analysis in the aftermath of insider threats. Detailed logs and historical telemetry allow security teams to recreate events down to the keystroke, showing exactly what happened, when, and by whom. This information is invaluable for internal reviews, legal proceedings, and regulatory reporting. It also enables organizations to learn from incidents and refine their policies, detection rules, and training programs to prevent similar threats in the future. By capturing a complete and immutable record of endpoint activity, EDR provides the evidentiary foundation required to address insider threats comprehensively.

Ultimately, addressing insider threats requires a combination of technology, policy, and human insight. EDR platforms provide the technical capabilities to detect, investigate, and respond to threats with speed and precision. When paired with a culture of security awareness, clear behavioral policies, and cross-functional collaboration, these tools empower organizations to identify insider risks before they escalate into serious incidents. As threats continue to evolve and insiders remain a potent vector for data compromise and operational disruption, the role of EDR in mitigating these risks becomes increasingly vital. By leveraging EDR to its full potential, organizations can protect their assets from within and foster a secure, accountable working environment.

EDR and Supply Chain Attack Detection

Supply chain attacks have emerged as one of the most sophisticated and difficult-to-detect forms of cyber threats facing modern organizations. These attacks target the interconnected ecosystem of vendors, software providers, hardware manufacturers, and service partners that businesses rely on to operate. Rather than directly compromising a well-defended enterprise, adversaries infiltrate trusted third parties to deliver malicious payloads or gain unauthorized access through established channels. The subtlety and complexity of such attacks mean they often evade traditional perimeter defenses and exploit the implicit trust granted to external entities. In this evolving threat landscape, Endpoint Detection and Response platforms have become critical tools in identifying and containing supply chain attacks, thanks to their unique ability to monitor endpoint behavior, detect anomalous activity, and correlate events across disparate systems in real time.

A hallmark of supply chain attacks is their use of legitimate processes and tools to execute malicious actions. Attackers may compromise a software update mechanism, insert backdoors into commonly used applications, or manipulate drivers and firmware during manufacturing. When deployed, these tainted components function normally, gaining the trust of users and administrators alike, while silently executing malicious routines in the background. This deceptive strategy makes it especially difficult for signature-based detection methods to identify the threat, as there are no conventional indicators of compromise at the time of deployment. EDR platforms overcome this limitation by focusing on behavior rather than static signatures. They observe how software behaves once it is installed, regardless of its origin, looking for patterns that indicate misuse, privilege escalation, lateral movement, or unauthorized data access.

One of the primary advantages of EDR in detecting supply chain attacks is its visibility into the entire execution lifecycle of applications and processes. When a malicious component is introduced through a compromised software update, it will eventually perform actions that deviate from expected behavior. This may include spawning unexpected processes, making unauthorized registry changes, injecting code into system memory, or establishing outbound

147

connections to suspicious command-and-control servers. EDR solutions log and analyze these actions continuously, enabling security analysts to detect deviations from the norm and investigate them further. This level of visibility allows defenders to identify the malicious behavior even if the initial delivery mechanism was trusted.

Supply chain attacks often unfold slowly over time, with attackers taking deliberate steps to remain undetected. They may install remote access tools, create new user accounts, or alter security settings to pave the way for future exploitation. EDR platforms help uncover this creeping compromise by correlating historical activity with current events. An analyst might notice that a system process began exhibiting abnormal behavior several weeks after a particular software package was installed. The EDR platform provides the telemetry needed to trace this activity back to its origin, linking seemingly benign installations to later-stage malicious actions. This retrospective analysis is vital in detecting supply chain compromises that only manifest long after initial delivery.

In addition to behavioral analysis, EDR platforms enhance supply chain attack detection by integrating with threat intelligence feeds. These feeds include data on known malicious domains, IP addresses, file hashes, and behavior patterns associated with advanced persistent threat groups. When an EDR agent observes a process communicating with a known malicious domain or executing code linked to a recent supply chain campaign, it can generate alerts for immediate investigation. This real-time threat correlation adds another layer of detection and strengthens the ability to catch emerging threats that exploit trusted relationships and third-party software dependencies.

Supply chain attacks also pose a challenge in terms of lateral movement. Once attackers establish a foothold on one endpoint, they often seek to expand their access across the network. EDR tools are designed to detect and prevent such lateral movement by monitoring for the use of remote administrative tools, credential theft techniques, and unusual inter-process communication. When an endpoint starts accessing systems it never previously communicated with, or when it attempts to move through network paths not associated with its role, the EDR solution can flag this behavior and take pre-defined response actions. By catching these movements early, security teams can contain the breach and prevent it from spreading to critical infrastructure.

Response capabilities are another crucial element of EDR effectiveness in managing supply chain threats. Once malicious behavior is detected, the EDR platform can automate containment actions, such as isolating the affected endpoint from the network, terminating suspicious processes, or rolling back unauthorized changes. These capabilities allow organizations to react quickly, minimizing the window of opportunity for attackers and reducing the potential impact. Furthermore, EDR solutions maintain a full forensic timeline of events, enabling incident responders to reconstruct the attack, identify the entry point, and understand the scope of the compromise. This evidence is essential not only for internal recovery but also for fulfilling legal, regulatory, and contractual obligations related to third-party risk management.

The importance of EDR in supply chain attack detection also extends to proactive defense. By continuously monitoring third-party applications and their behavior across endpoints, organizations can identify patterns of risk before a breach occurs. If multiple endpoints begin experiencing anomalies following the deployment of a particular software update, the EDR platform can highlight this correlation, prompting further investigation and potentially leading to the identification of a compromised supplier. This proactive approach supports a broader risk management strategy, enabling organizations to assess the security posture of their vendors based on real operational data rather than relying solely on questionnaires or periodic audits.

Moreover, the role of EDR in defending against supply chain threats aligns with industry best practices for Zero Trust architectures. In a Zero Trust model, no user or system is implicitly trusted, even if it resides within the traditional network perimeter. EDR tools enforce this principle by continuously evaluating endpoint behavior and validating trust through real-time analysis. Even software from reputable vendors is subject to the same scrutiny as unknown applications. This consistent application of security controls helps neutralize the risk introduced by third-party relationships and ensures that trust is earned through verification, not assumed.

As supply chain attacks become more frequent, targeted, and damaging, the need for advanced detection and response capabilities has never been greater. Traditional defenses that rely on static rules and perimeter-based monitoring are insufficient against adversaries who exploit the trust between organizations and their partners. EDR platforms provide a dynamic, behavior-based approach that identifies threats based on what software and users do, not just who they are or where they came from. By combining real-time telemetry, automated response, historical analysis, and threat intelligence integration, EDR solutions empower organizations to detect and contain supply chain attacks before they cause irreparable harm. In an interconnected world where trust can be weaponized, EDR serves as a critical line of defense that ensures visibility, accountability, and resilience across the entire endpoint ecosystem.

Mobile Device Endpoint Detection Challenges

The rapid proliferation of mobile devices in the workplace has fundamentally changed the nature of endpoint security. Smartphones and tablets have become essential tools for modern business operations, providing employees with the ability to work from anywhere, access sensitive data on the go, and remain connected at all times. However, this convenience comes at a cost. Mobile devices, by their very nature, present a unique and evolving set of challenges for endpoint detection. Unlike traditional endpoints such as desktops and laptops, mobile devices operate on different architectures, rely on distinct operating systems, and exist in highly dynamic usage environments. These differences introduce numerous obstacles for security teams attempting to deploy and manage effective Endpoint Detection and Response strategies for mobile endpoints.

One of the most significant challenges in detecting threats on mobile devices is the restricted visibility imposed by the operating systems themselves. Both iOS and Android are designed with security and user privacy in mind, which limits the access that third-party applications, including security tools, have to system-level data. On iOS, sandboxing and the lack of access to system logs prevent traditional EDR agents from observing process behavior, memory usage, or kernel-level activity. On Android, while the level of access is slightly more flexible, particularly on rooted devices, the diversity of hardware vendors and operating system versions creates inconsistencies in the telemetry that can be collected. These architectural limitations mean that many of the techniques used in traditional EDR, such as process tracing or file integrity monitoring, cannot be implemented in the same way on mobile devices.

Another major challenge is the transient and decentralized nature of mobile connectivity. Unlike fixed desktops that are always connected to the corporate network, mobile devices constantly shift between different networks, including home Wi-Fi, public hotspots, and cellular data. This variability in network environment makes it difficult for centralized EDR systems to maintain persistent communication with mobile endpoints or to reliably capture traffic for analysis. Attackers can exploit this mobility to launch network-based attacks when the device is outside the protective reach of enterprise firewalls or VPNs. Furthermore, mobile endpoints are frequently powered off, out of coverage, or otherwise unavailable, creating blind spots in the security team's visibility and reducing the effectiveness of continuous monitoring strategies.

The variety and fragmentation of mobile device ecosystems also complicate endpoint detection efforts. Android alone encompasses hundreds of manufacturers and thousands of device models, each with unique configurations, security patch levels, and custom firmware. This fragmentation introduces inconsistency in how security features are implemented and maintained, resulting in uneven protection across the device fleet. Security teams must account for a broad range of scenarios, from fully managed and secured corporate devices to bring-your-own-device endpoints running outdated operating systems and third-party applications. This complexity makes it difficult to deploy a uniform EDR solution and increases the likelihood that some devices will remain vulnerable or unmonitored.

Mobile applications themselves present another vector of concern. Unlike traditional desktop applications that are often tightly controlled within enterprise environments, mobile apps are downloaded from app stores that may not rigorously vet submissions or detect obfuscated malware. Malicious apps can disguise themselves as legitimate productivity tools or exploit permissions granted by unsuspecting users to access sensitive data, record keystrokes, or exfiltrate information. Detecting such threats on mobile endpoints is challenging because EDR tools cannot always analyze app behavior in depth or inspect encrypted communications. Additionally, the use of sideloaded applications or third-party app stores further increases the attack surface and complicates detection efforts.

User behavior and privacy expectations play a crucial role in shaping mobile endpoint detection capabilities. Mobile devices are inherently personal, and users are often more sensitive to the idea of being monitored. Security tools that are too intrusive risk violating user privacy or running afoul of data protection regulations. This is especially true in bring-your-own-device environments, where corporate security teams must balance visibility and control with respect for the user's personal data and applications. As a result, EDR tools must be carefully designed to collect only necessary data, anonymize sensitive information when possible, and operate transparently to maintain user trust. This balancing act can limit the depth of telemetry collected and reduce the effectiveness of threat detection, especially when malicious activity mimics normal user behavior.

Battery life and device performance are also critical considerations. Mobile users expect their devices to function smoothly and maintain battery charge throughout the day. EDR solutions that consume too much power or processing resources may be disabled by users or restricted by the operating system's power management policies. This constraint forces vendors to develop lightweight agents that minimize their impact on the device, but it also limits the scope and frequency of data collection. Security teams must therefore rely on optimized data collection techniques, intelligent sampling, and cloud-based analytics to fill the gaps without degrading the user experience.

Another layer of complexity comes from the integration of mobile devices into enterprise cloud services and productivity platforms. Modern mobile endpoints frequently interact with corporate resources through SaaS applications, virtual desktops, and file synchronization services. While this integration increases productivity, it also creates indirect paths for data leakage and unauthorized access. EDR solutions must be capable of correlating mobile endpoint activity with cloud service usage, identifying anomalies such as data downloads from unexpected locations, or logins from devices not previously associated with the user. Achieving this level of correlation often requires integration with Mobile Device Management platforms, cloud access security brokers, and identity and access management systems.

Developing effective response strategies for mobile threats presents additional challenges. Traditional response actions such as isolating a device from the network, terminating malicious processes, or collecting memory snapshots are not always feasible on mobile platforms. Operating systems may not support such controls, and user ownership of the device may limit what actions can legally or ethically be taken. As a result, containment and remediation efforts often rely on indirect methods, such as pushing device lock commands through mobile management systems, revoking access tokens, or prompting the user to uninstall suspicious applications. These response mechanisms are less immediate and less precise than those available for traditional endpoints, which can allow threats to persist longer or spread to other systems.

Despite these challenges, the importance of securing mobile endpoints continues to grow. As mobile devices become more integral to business operations and attackers adapt their techniques to target these platforms, the need for robust, adaptive, and privacy-conscious detection mechanisms is critical. EDR vendors are increasingly investing in mobile-specific solutions that leverage modern techniques such as anomaly detection, behavioral analytics, and machine learning to enhance threat visibility. Some solutions use cloud-side analysis to offload heavy processing, while others rely on OS-level integrations with mobile platforms to gain deeper access without violating system integrity.

Securing mobile endpoints requires a new mindset and a collaborative approach between security teams, IT operations, end users, and software vendors. While traditional EDR principles still apply, they must be reimagined to fit the constraints and realities of the mobile landscape. Visibility must be achieved without intrusion, detection must operate under limited access, and response must be both effective and respectful of user boundaries. As mobile threats continue to evolve, organizations must embrace this complexity and work to build endpoint detection strategies that reflect the true diversity and dynamism of the devices that now define the modern workplace.

IoT Endpoint Protection Strategies

The proliferation of Internet of Things devices across industries has dramatically expanded the attack surface of modern enterprises. IoT endpoints now include everything from industrial control systems and medical devices to smart cameras, environmental sensors, and connected appliances. While these devices offer operational efficiency, automation, and data-driven decision-making, they also introduce unique security challenges. Traditional security tools, including standard Endpoint Detection and Response platforms, are often ill-equipped to manage the scale, diversity, and limitations of IoT environments. Crafting effective IoT endpoint protection strategies requires a nuanced understanding of how these devices function, the threats they face, and the methods by which they can be monitored and defended without disrupting their core purposes.

One of the primary challenges in securing IoT endpoints stems from their inherent design constraints. Many IoT devices are built for specific tasks and operate with minimal computing power, limited memory, and constrained operating systems. These resource limitations make it difficult or impossible to install traditional security agents or run complex detection algorithms locally. Unlike desktops and servers, which can support full-scale EDR clients that collect telemetry, analyze behavior, and execute automated responses, IoT devices often lack the capability to do any of these tasks internally. As a result, security teams must find alternative methods for monitoring and protecting these endpoints without placing additional burden on their performance or stability.

Another complication arises from the diversity of IoT devices and protocols. Enterprises often deploy IoT solutions from multiple vendors, each with its own firmware, communication standards, update mechanisms, and security models. Devices may operate on proprietary protocols, communicate intermittently, or rely on cloud-based backends maintained by third parties. This fragmentation makes it difficult to establish uniform visibility or enforce consistent security policies. Some devices may support basic security features like firmware signing or encrypted communication, while others may lack even password protection. A one-size-fits-all security solution is therefore impractical, and organizations must instead adopt layered strategies that consider the capabilities and risks associated with each class of device.

Visibility remains a cornerstone of any effective IoT security strategy. Since direct telemetry collection is often not feasible, security teams must rely on alternative data sources to gain insight into device behavior. Network traffic analysis becomes especially important, as it can reveal anomalous communication patterns, unexpected outbound connections, or unusual protocol usage. By deploying network sensors or leveraging existing network infrastructure such as firewalls and switches, organizations can build a profile of normal behavior for each type of IoT device and flag deviations for further investigation. This approach allows for the detection of compromised devices or unauthorized firmware changes without requiring access to the devices themselves.

Segmentation is another key strategy in IoT endpoint protection. Given the limitations of on-device security, isolating IoT endpoints from critical systems and data is essential. Network segmentation ensures that even if an IoT device is compromised, its ability to spread malware, exfiltrate data, or interfere with operations is limited. Microsegmentation, which restricts device communication to only what is necessary for its function, further reduces risk. For instance, a smart thermostat should not have the ability to communicate with an enterprise database server. Enforcing these boundaries requires careful planning, documentation, and the use of technologies such as VLANs, firewalls, and software-defined networking solutions. When combined with continuous monitoring, segmentation not only reduces the blast radius of an attack but also makes it easier to detect lateral movement attempts originating from IoT devices.

Access control mechanisms are critical in securing IoT endpoints. Default credentials, weak passwords, and lack of authentication are common vulnerabilities that attackers exploit. Every device must be configured with unique credentials, and wherever possible, multi-factor authentication and certificate-based access should be employed. Devices should also be provisioned according to the principle of least privilege, granting them only the access necessary for their function. Managing credentials at scale can be challenging, particularly in environments with thousands of IoT devices, but this can be addressed through integration with identity and access management platforms or IoT-specific device management solutions that automate credential rotation and enforce security baselines.

Firmware and software updates present a significant opportunity and a major challenge in IoT security. Many vulnerabilities in IoT devices stem from outdated or unpatched firmware. However, the update mechanisms for IoT devices are often poorly implemented or nonexistent. Some devices require manual updates through physical connections, while others rely on the vendor to push updates remotely, with little visibility or control on the customer's side. To address this, organizations must establish rigorous asset inventory and vulnerability management processes that track firmware versions, vendor support lifecycles, and known vulnerabilities. Where possible, devices should be selected based on their support for secure update protocols, and vendors should be held accountable for maintaining regular patch cycles and providing transparency around vulnerabilities and mitigations.

Anomaly detection and threat intelligence are increasingly being integrated into IoT protection strategies. By correlating behavior observed across multiple devices and comparing it to known threat patterns, security platforms can detect coordinated attacks or widespread vulnerabilities. For example, if multiple surveillance cameras begin communicating with unfamiliar IP addresses or exhibiting sudden spikes in outbound traffic, this could indicate participation in a botnet or an ongoing data exfiltration campaign. Cloud-based threat intelligence platforms can aggregate such observations from many organizations, enabling faster identification of emerging threats. Feeding this intelligence into existing detection and response workflows ensures that IoT-specific threats are not overlooked simply because they originate from unconventional endpoints.

Incident response in IoT environments requires adaptation as well. Traditional responses such as quarantining or reimaging may not be feasible or sufficient for IoT devices. Instead, organizations must be prepared to isolate devices at the network level, disable specific functions remotely, or physically remove them from the environment in extreme cases. Having pre-defined playbooks for different IoT threat scenarios improves response time and coordination across security, IT, and operational technology teams. Clear communication channels with device vendors and service providers are also necessary, as many remediation actions depend on external cooperation.

Ultimately, protecting IoT endpoints is not about replicating traditional endpoint security approaches, but about rethinking them. The goal is to create a framework of layered defenses that compensate for the inherent weaknesses of IoT devices while enabling their safe and reliable operation. This includes a combination of asset visibility, network controls, behavioral monitoring, access management, secure provisioning, and response readiness. As IoT continues to integrate more deeply into critical business processes and infrastructure, the importance of tailored endpoint protection strategies will only grow. Organizations that proactively address these challenges and build resilient, adaptive security frameworks will be better positioned to harness the full potential of IoT without compromising safety, privacy, or operational continuity.

Continuous Improvement in EDR Operations

The dynamic nature of cybersecurity threats demands a mindset of continuous improvement in every aspect of defensive operations, and Endpoint Detection and Response is no exception. As attackers evolve their tactics, techniques, and procedures, EDR operations must evolve in parallel, adapting to new threat patterns, refining detection logic, optimizing workflows, and expanding visibility. An effective EDR strategy is not static; it is a living, iterative process that incorporates feedback, intelligence, and lessons learned to become more effective over time. Continuous improvement in EDR operations requires a structured yet flexible approach, combining technical enhancements, procedural refinement, human skill development, and strategic alignment with the organization's broader security objectives.

One of the fundamental pillars of continuous improvement in EDR is the refinement of detection capabilities. When an EDR solution is first deployed, it typically begins with a set of predefined detection rules and behavioral baselines. While these are effective in identifying common threats, they may not capture the nuances of a specific organization's environment or the unique threats it faces. Over time, security teams must customize and tune these detection rules to better reflect their operational context. This includes modifying thresholds, excluding known benign behaviors, and creating new detection logic based on internal threat hunting efforts and incident postmortems. Each detection that proves valuable should be analyzed for generalization, asking whether similar activities can be caught earlier or across a broader range of endpoints.

False positives and false negatives are constant challenges in EDR operations, and minimizing both is essential for improving accuracy and analyst efficiency. Each alert should be evaluated not only for its immediate threat value but also for its underlying quality. If an alert turns out to be benign, the detection logic should be reviewed to determine whether it is too sensitive or lacks context. If a threat goes undetected until damage is done, analysts should determine why the detection failed and what signals were missed. These reviews must feed directly into detection engineering processes, with updated rules deployed promptly and tested against relevant scenarios to ensure efficacy. This feedback loop reduces noise over time and ensures that the most meaningful alerts receive the attention they deserve.

Detection logic alone is not enough without effective response workflows. Continuous improvement also applies to how alerts are triaged, escalated, and resolved. This involves regularly evaluating incident response playbooks to ensure they remain current, comprehensive, and aligned with emerging threats. Playbooks should be reviewed after every significant incident, with input from all involved stakeholders. Were the steps followed correctly? Did they result in timely containment and remediation? Were there delays or ambiguities? Any identified shortcomings should be addressed through revisions to documentation, updates to automation scripts, or adjustments in team responsibilities. Playbook testing through tabletop exercises or red team simulations further supports the refinement of response procedures, helping to identify gaps before they are exploited by real adversaries.

Analyst training and development are also central to the process of EDR improvement. Even the most advanced platform will fall short if the people using it are not equipped with the knowledge and experience required to extract its full value. Ongoing training programs should include both technical instruction on using the EDR platform and broader education in threat analysis, malware behavior, and digital forensics. Analysts should be encouraged to participate in external threat intelligence communities, attend cybersecurity conferences, and earn relevant certifications. Internal knowledge sharing should be promoted through post-incident reviews, collaborative hunt sessions, and shared documentation. By cultivating a skilled and engaged analyst team, organizations ensure that their EDR operations are not only effective but also resilient in the face of change.

Another driver of continuous improvement is the integration of threat intelligence into EDR workflows. Intelligence about new threats, emerging vulnerabilities, and attacker tactics can significantly enhance detection and response efforts. EDR platforms should be configured to ingest threat intelligence feeds, whether from commercial providers, open-source communities, or government sharing initiatives. These feeds can enrich alerts with context, trigger new detection rules, or guide threat hunting efforts. However, this integration must be actively managed. Not all intelligence is equally valuable, and the relevance of each feed should be periodically reviewed. Organizations should track how often each source contributes to actual detections or investigations and adjust subscriptions accordingly.

Metrics and analytics provide the foundation for measuring progress and guiding future improvements. Security teams should define and track a set of key performance indicators that reflect the health and effectiveness of EDR operations. These might include mean time to detect, mean time to respond, alert-to-incident conversion rate, number of incidents resolved per analyst, and the percentage of endpoints covered by the EDR solution. Regular reporting on these metrics helps identify trends, benchmark performance, and justify investments in additional tools, training, or personnel. When anomalies are identified—such as a sudden increase in undetected threats or a drop in response efficiency—they should prompt root cause analysis and corrective action.

Automation is another area ripe for continuous improvement. As organizations mature in their use of EDR, they often begin to automate more elements of their detection and response processes. This can include automated alert enrichment, risk scoring, playbook execution, and even basic investigation steps such as gathering logs or querying endpoint data. Automation must be carefully monitored and regularly tested to ensure it behaves as expected and remains aligned with evolving threats and policies. Opportunities for further automation should be identified through process reviews and time tracking exercises that reveal repetitive or manual tasks that could be handled by scripts or orchestration platforms.

Finally, strategic alignment ensures that EDR operations continue to support the organization's mission and adapt to its changing needs. Business priorities, regulatory requirements, and risk tolerance levels evolve over time, and EDR strategy must evolve with them. Security leaders must engage with executive stakeholders to ensure EDR efforts are informed by business context and that any changes in the business environment are reflected in security planning. For example, a shift toward remote work or cloud-based infrastructure may necessitate new detection rules, additional data sources, or revised access controls. Regular strategy reviews, aligned with business planning cycles, help ensure that EDR investments remain focused, relevant, and impactful.

Continuous improvement in EDR operations is not a destination but a journey. It requires a culture of curiosity, accountability, and adaptability. It demands that every incident be treated as a learning opportunity, every alert as a signal for tuning, and every new threat as a challenge to be met with better tools, smarter processes, and more informed people. In a landscape where threats evolve daily and the cost of failure is high, the organizations that thrive will be those that embrace change, seek feedback relentlessly, and commit to refining their EDR capabilities at every level. This mindset transforms EDR from a static tool into a dynamic, strategic asset that strengthens the organization's ability to detect, respond, and recover from even the most sophisticated attacks.

Threat Containment Metrics and KPIs

Threat containment is a critical function within any Endpoint Detection and Response strategy. It marks the point where detection gives way to action, and the effectiveness of this transition determines whether an incident becomes a contained disruption or escalates into a damaging breach. Measuring how well an organization performs in this area requires the use of well-defined metrics and key performance indicators. These measurements serve as both diagnostic tools and benchmarks, allowing security teams to assess performance, uncover inefficiencies, justify investments, and drive continuous improvement. The development and implementation of containment metrics and KPIs are not just technical exercises; they are strategic imperatives that guide the evolution of a security program and demonstrate its value to the broader organization.

One of the most foundational metrics for evaluating threat containment is Mean Time to Contain, often abbreviated as MTTC. This metric tracks the average time between the detection of a threat and the successful execution of containment actions. It measures the agility of the security team and the efficiency of their processes. A lower MTTC typically indicates a well-tuned detection and response pipeline, where alerts are prioritized appropriately, decisions are made swiftly, and response tools are used effectively. High MTTC values, on the other hand, may signal bottlenecks in alert triage, unclear escalation paths, or limitations in response tooling. MTTC is a central metric that reflects the core purpose of containment: to minimize the window in which a threat can move, expand, or cause damage.

Another key metric is Containment Rate, which measures the percentage of detected threats that were successfully contained before causing further impact. This metric can be broken down by threat type, severity level, or endpoint category to provide deeper insight into the effectiveness of containment efforts across different dimensions. A high containment rate suggests that the organization is capable of rapidly and accurately neutralizing threats, while a low rate may indicate issues such as misconfigured tools, poor alert fidelity, or delays in decision-making. By correlating this metric with the source of the detection—whether it came from automated alerts, manual hunting, or external notification—security teams can assess the reliability of their detection ecosystem and identify gaps that need to be addressed.

Containment Coverage is another important KPI, especially in environments with a diverse and distributed endpoint population. This metric reflects the percentage of endpoints that are equipped with the necessary controls to execute containment actions. It measures the reach of EDR tooling and the completeness of deployment across the organization. For containment to be effective, every endpoint must be capable of being isolated, remediated, or otherwise controlled at the moment of need. Incomplete coverage introduces risk, as undetected or unmanaged endpoints can become pivot points for attackers. Tracking containment coverage ensures that the infrastructure is aligned with the organization's security architecture and that no endpoints are left vulnerable due to oversight or technical debt.

The Success Rate of Automated Containment is another valuable KPI. Automation plays an increasingly critical role in EDR operations, enabling fast response times and reducing reliance on manual intervention. This metric evaluates how often automated response actions—such as isolating a host, terminating a malicious process, or revoking user credentials—are executed as intended without failure or unintended consequences. It helps assess the reliability of automation scripts and the accuracy of playbook logic. A high success rate builds trust in automation and allows for broader use in future incidents, while a low success rate may prompt reviews of logic, environmental compatibility, or agent stability. Tracking this metric over time also supports the gradual expansion of automation into more complex response scenarios.

Containment Action Latency provides a more granular view of performance by measuring the time taken for each specific containment action once the decision to contain has been made. This includes the delay between issuing an isolation command and the endpoint being fully disconnected, or the lag between initiating process termination and the process ceasing execution. These measurements highlight the operational efficiency of the tools in use and the responsiveness of the network and endpoint infrastructure. Identifying high latency in containment actions may point to technical limitations such as network congestion, agent performance issues, or process locking conflicts that need to be resolved.

Another critical area for measurement is Containment Escalation Rate. This KPI tracks how often containment decisions are escalated to higher-tier analysts or incident response teams. While some escalation is expected, a high rate may indicate that initial containment parameters are too broad, that first responders lack the confidence or authority to act decisively, or that detection logic is generating ambiguous alerts. Reducing unnecessary escalations through better training, clearer playbooks, and more actionable alerts can significantly improve containment speed and reduce overall operational overhead.

Post-Containment Validation Rate measures how often containment actions are verified for effectiveness. Simply issuing a containment command does not guarantee that the threat has been neutralized. This metric assesses how frequently follow-up validation is performed, such as scanning the isolated endpoint, checking for lateral movement, or confirming that malicious processes were fully terminated. High validation rates are associated with mature response practices and increase confidence in the organization's containment outcomes. They also provide data for post-incident analysis and continuous improvement.

From a broader perspective, Business Impact Reduction due to Containment can be used to quantify the real-world value of containment efforts. This KPI estimates the reduction in operational disruption, data loss, or financial impact that results from timely containment. It requires collaboration with risk management and business continuity teams to develop models that translate technical outcomes into business metrics. This helps communicate the importance of containment to non-technical stakeholders and positions the security team as a key contributor to organizational resilience.

Containment metrics must also be contextualized with threat intelligence. Understanding how containment efforts align with known threat actor behaviors, MITRE ATT&CK techniques, and industry trends allows for better prioritization and more effective defenses. When threats detected and contained match patterns associated with high-profile adversaries, this indicates that the organization's containment strategy is keeping pace with the threat landscape. Conversely, if incidents frequently involve techniques that are not addressed in containment playbooks, this signals a need to update detection and response capabilities accordingly.

Finally, all containment metrics and KPIs should feed into a structured reporting and review process. Regular review cycles ensure that insights from metrics lead to action. This might involve monthly operations reviews, quarterly executive summaries, or real-time dashboards shared with key stakeholders. These reports drive accountability, highlight successes, and surface areas for investment or improvement. By embedding metrics into the operational rhythm of the security organization, containment efforts are no longer reactive measures taken in crisis but become proactive elements of a disciplined, data-driven security program that continually adapts to meet the challenges of a dynamic threat environment.

Building an EDR Incident Response Team

Establishing a dedicated Endpoint Detection and Response incident response team is a critical investment in an organization's ability to defend itself against rapidly evolving cyber threats. As cyberattacks grow more sophisticated and frequent, traditional perimeter-based defenses are no longer sufficient to prevent or contain breaches. Instead, organizations must rely on highly skilled teams capable of monitoring endpoint activity, detecting anomalies, analyzing malicious behaviors, and executing rapid response actions when threats are identified. Building such a team requires more than hiring a few technically proficient analysts. It demands a carefully structured approach that combines clear roles and responsibilities, continuous training, well-defined workflows, tool proficiency, and interdepartmental collaboration.

The foundation of an effective EDR incident response team lies in its structure and the clarity of its operational scope. Teams must be designed to align with the organization's size, complexity, and industry-specific risk profile. In larger enterprises, this might involve multiple tiers of analysts, each responsible for different aspects of the response lifecycle. Tier one analysts handle initial alert triage and escalate confirmed threats. Tier two analysts investigate complex incidents, perform root cause analysis, and execute containment. Tier three or senior analysts focus on threat hunting, detection engineering, and post-incident reviews. In smaller organizations, roles may be consolidated, but the need for coverage across the entire response spectrum remains the same.

Team members must possess a diverse set of technical and analytical skills. Deep familiarity with operating systems, especially Windows and Linux, is essential for interpreting endpoint telemetry. Analysts should understand how processes interact, how memory is allocated, how logs are generated, and how attackers exploit native tools to evade detection. Proficiency with scripting languages such as Python or PowerShell enhances an analyst's ability to automate tasks, extract data, and conduct advanced investigations. A strong grasp of networking fundamentals is also necessary, as many endpoint detections are tied to suspicious network behavior. Beyond technical skills, analysts need critical thinking, pattern recognition, and an investigative mindset that allows them to piece together fragmented indicators and uncover the broader narrative of an attack.

Tool proficiency is another vital element. The team must be intimately familiar with the capabilities, limitations, and workflows of the chosen EDR platform. This includes understanding how telemetry is collected and stored, how alerts are generated, how to search historical data, and how to use the platform's response functions such as host isolation, process termination, or file quarantine. Analysts should also be comfortable integrating the EDR solution with other tools such as SIEMs, SOAR platforms, and threat intelligence feeds. Regular training sessions, hands-on exercises, and simulation environments help ensure that team members can respond effectively under pressure and remain current with evolving platform features.

Communication is a crucial but often overlooked component of incident response. The EDR team must communicate effectively both within the security function and with stakeholders across the organization. During an incident, clear communication protocols help avoid confusion, ensure timely escalation, and maintain a consistent narrative across technical and executive audiences. This requires the development of communication playbooks that define who needs to be informed, when, and with what level of detail. Analysts should be trained to document their findings clearly, justify their conclusions with evidence, and present information in a way that supports decision-making by IT, legal, compliance, and executive teams. Post-incident debriefs, or after-action reviews, offer valuable opportunities to improve communication practices based on real-world experience.

To sustain long-term effectiveness, an EDR incident response team must operate within a framework of continuous improvement. This involves regular assessments of detection coverage, incident response performance, and workflow efficiency. Metrics such as mean time to detect, mean time to contain, false positive rates, and analyst workload provide insights into operational health and help identify areas for optimization. Feedback loops should be built into every stage of the incident lifecycle, enabling the team to refine detection rules, update response playbooks, and adjust staffing or training as needed. Lessons learned from each incident must be documented and translated into actionable changes, ensuring that mistakes are not repeated and successes are institutionalized.

Cross-functional collaboration enhances the impact of the EDR incident response team. Security teams must work closely with IT operations to implement containment actions, apply patches, or restore systems. Coordination with legal and compliance teams is necessary when incidents involve regulatory or contractual implications. Human resources may need to be involved if insider threats or employee misconduct is suspected. These relationships must be established before incidents occur, supported by clear escalation paths, shared documentation, and mutual understanding of roles and responsibilities. The EDR team can also benefit from input provided by business units, which helps contextualize endpoint behavior and prioritize response based on the criticality of affected systems or data.

Another important consideration in building an EDR incident response team is staffing continuity and coverage. Threats can emerge at any time, and response teams must be prepared to act around the clock. This may require implementing a follow-the-sun model, rotating on-call duties, or partnering with managed detection and response providers to ensure consistent coverage. Burnout is a real risk in high-pressure security environments, and team leaders must take steps to manage workloads, provide psychological support, and promote work-life balance. Investing in the well-being of analysts is not just ethical but strategic, as it preserves institutional knowledge and sustains team morale and performance over time.

Developing a strong culture of security within the EDR team and the organization as a whole reinforces the team's effectiveness. Team members should be encouraged to take ownership of their work, share knowledge, and contribute to the evolution of tools and processes. Recognition of individual and team achievements boosts engagement and helps attract and retain top talent. Security awareness initiatives across the broader organization also support the team's mission by reducing the number of preventable incidents and improving the quality of incident reporting from users.

The establishment of an EDR incident response team represents a deliberate and strategic effort to build a mature, capable defense against endpoint threats. It is a multifaceted endeavor that blends technical skill, operational rigor, and organizational alignment. By clearly defining roles, investing in training, cultivating communication, measuring performance, and fostering collaboration, organizations can create a responsive, resilient team capable of detecting and containing threats before they cause harm. As endpoint attacks grow in scale and complexity, this team becomes not just a reactive force but a proactive guardian of enterprise security, essential to the integrity and continuity of business operations.

Case Studies of EDR in Action

Real-world case studies offer a powerful lens through which to understand the value and application of Endpoint Detection and Response solutions. While theoretical discussions and technical specifications provide important context, it is the practical use of EDR tools during active security incidents that reveals their true capabilities. Organizations across different industries and sizes have faced diverse threats, and their experiences in deploying EDR platforms during times of crisis illustrate the range of outcomes that these technologies can enable. From rapid containment of ransomware to uncovering sophisticated insider threats, the following scenarios reflect how EDR tools have become essential assets in cybersecurity operations.

One major multinational manufacturing company faced a targeted ransomware attack that originated through a phishing email opened by a senior employee. The malicious attachment deployed a remote access trojan which remained dormant for several days before launching a script that began encrypting files across the network. Fortunately, the organization had recently deployed an EDR platform across all workstations and servers. As soon as the malware initiated lateral movement and file modifications outside of standard user behavior, the EDR solution flagged the anomaly and generated high-priority alerts. Analysts were able to review the process tree, observe the parent-child relationship between the email client and the script, and identify the full scope of compromised machines. The EDR platform's containment capabilities allowed the security team to isolate affected endpoints from the network in real time, halting the spread of the ransomware. Through forensic analysis facilitated by the EDR tool, the security team traced the initial compromise back to the phishing email and implemented additional email filtering rules and user awareness training as a preventive measure. The entire containment operation, from detection to isolation, occurred within hours, limiting damage to fewer than five endpoints and avoiding operational downtime.

In a different scenario, a large financial services firm discovered signs of a possible insider threat after a mid-level employee accessed sensitive client data outside of normal business hours. The firm's EDR platform recorded the anomalous file access and generated an alert based on behavior that deviated from the user's established baseline. Upon investigation, the EDR console revealed that the employee had used unauthorized scripts to extract large volumes of data and attempted to upload them to a personal cloud storage account. The platform's detailed forensic timeline allowed analysts to reconstruct the incident, showing when and how the data was accessed, which processes were used, and the sequence of exfiltration attempts. The response team used the EDR solution to remotely terminate the processes and block further file transfers, while HR and legal departments were brought in to manage the internal disciplinary response. This case highlighted the value of behavioral analytics within EDR and the importance of visibility at the process level. Without such a solution, the activity could have remained hidden until much greater damage had been done or regulatory violations had occurred.

A government agency dealing with critical infrastructure faced a more complex and prolonged attack involving an advanced persistent threat group. The attackers had gained access through a vulnerable third-party application and had been operating inside the network for weeks before their presence was noticed. The agency's EDR system began correlating subtle signals from multiple endpoints, including anomalous registry changes, uncommon command-line executions, and unusual remote desktop connections initiated during off-hours. Analysts used the platform's hunting capabilities to query these behaviors across thousands of devices and gradually built a picture of the attacker's lateral movement. The ability to pivot across endpoints and correlate telemetry over time proved crucial in understanding the full scope of the compromise. While some systems had to be taken offline temporarily, the EDR system enabled a surgical response that avoided widespread disruption. The agency coordinated with national cyber defense authorities and used intelligence gathered during the investigation to contribute to the broader understanding of the threat actor's tools and tactics. This case demonstrated the power of EDR tools not only in stopping active threats but also in contributing to global threat intelligence sharing and long-term security posture improvement.

Another illustrative example comes from a healthcare provider that relied heavily on cloud applications and a hybrid IT infrastructure.

After a user's credentials were stolen through a spear-phishing attack, the attacker began probing internal systems, searching for unprotected data repositories. The EDR solution immediately detected suspicious PowerShell commands issued by the attacker and flagged them due to their deviation from the user's normal activity and known benign scripts. Because the organization had integrated its EDR with a SOAR platform, the detection automatically triggered a response playbook. The playbook initiated endpoint isolation, notified security analysts, and gathered logs from the affected machine. Within minutes, analysts had full visibility into the attack, including the source IP, the command execution sequence, and the attacker's attempts to bypass group policy restrictions. The rapid containment prevented the exposure of any patient data and allowed the organization to meet its compliance obligations without issuing breach notifications. The automated response capabilities, combined with real-time telemetry, provided a compelling example of how EDR and orchestration platforms can work together to reduce time-to-response dramatically.

In the realm of education, a large university experienced a cryptomining outbreak across several student-access lab machines. The mining scripts were disguised as legitimate system utilities and were scheduled to run during idle periods to avoid detection. The EDR platform, however, identified the unusual CPU usage patterns and alerted the security team. By examining the process lineage and scheduled task configurations, analysts quickly identified the malicious scripts and their distribution method. The university's IT staff used the EDR console to deploy removal scripts across all affected endpoints and blocked the attacker's command-and-control IP addresses at the firewall. The event prompted a broader review of endpoint policies and led to the implementation of stricter application control and scheduled task monitoring.

These case studies illustrate the diverse ways in which EDR solutions can be leveraged to identify, contain, and investigate threats across a wide range of operational environments. Whether responding to ransomware, insider threats, persistent attackers, credential misuse, or resource hijacking, EDR platforms have demonstrated their ability to provide deep visibility, actionable intelligence, and swift containment mechanisms. Their value is not confined to reactive defense; they also support proactive measures, compliance, and organizational learning.

By capturing detailed telemetry and enabling real-time response, EDR tools empower organizations to shift from being passive targets to active defenders capable of anticipating, identifying, and mitigating cyber threats in a timely and coordinated manner. The success of these responses hinges not only on the technology itself but on the readiness of the teams who use it, the clarity of their processes, and the integration of EDR into the broader cybersecurity strategy.

EDR and Ransomware Mitigation Tactics

Ransomware has evolved into one of the most disruptive and costly cyber threats affecting organizations across every industry. The modern ransomware ecosystem is highly organized, with attackers deploying increasingly sophisticated techniques to penetrate environments, escalate privileges, encrypt or exfiltrate sensitive data, and demand high-value ransoms. Traditional security measures, such as signature-based antivirus and perimeter firewalls, are often inadequate in detecting or stopping ransomware in its early stages. This is where Endpoint Detection and Response platforms become a vital component of any ransomware mitigation strategy. EDR solutions offer continuous visibility, behavioral analysis, and real-time response capabilities that empower security teams to detect ransomware activity early, contain its spread, and preserve forensic data necessary for post-incident analysis and recovery.

Ransomware attacks typically unfold in several stages, beginning with initial access, often via phishing emails, malicious attachments, compromised credentials, or vulnerable internet-facing services. Once inside the network, attackers seek to establish persistence, perform reconnaissance, escalate privileges, and ultimately deploy the encryption payload. EDR platforms are uniquely suited to disrupt this chain of attack at multiple points. During initial access, EDR solutions monitor process activity and network behavior, flagging anomalies such as unusual command-line arguments, execution of known malicious binaries, or unauthorized PowerShell usage. Early detection of these actions provides a critical window of opportunity to interrupt the attacker's progress before encryption begins.

A key tactic in ransomware mitigation with EDR is behavioral detection. Unlike traditional antivirus tools that rely on known file signatures, EDR platforms detect malicious activity based on behavior that deviates from baseline norms. Ransomware operations often involve abnormal file access patterns, including rapid file reads and writes, renaming or deletion of files, and creation of large numbers of encrypted files with unusual extensions. EDR agents monitor these patterns and trigger alerts when thresholds are exceeded or when behaviors match known ransomware profiles. This allows for early identification of ransomware in action, even if the specific strain is previously unknown or has been obfuscated to avoid signature detection.

EDR platforms also play a crucial role in lateral movement detection, which is a common tactic used by ransomware operators to spread across networks and encrypt as many systems as possible. Techniques such as pass-the-hash, remote desktop protocol abuse, and Windows Management Instrumentation can be used to traverse the environment. EDR tools log these activities in detail, capturing the context of the initiating process, the user involved, and the target system. This telemetry enables analysts to quickly trace the path of the attacker, identify compromised credentials, and stop further movement. Containment actions such as network isolation of endpoints, forced logoff of user accounts, or revocation of authentication tokens can be executed directly from the EDR console, halting the attacker's progress in real time.

Another effective EDR tactic for ransomware mitigation is process and script blocking. Security teams can configure their EDR platforms to deny execution of known malicious binaries or prevent high-risk tools such as certain scripting languages, command-line utilities, and file compression software from executing without proper authorization. These policies are particularly useful in environments where users have broad access privileges or where controls on software installation are limited. EDR tools can also detect and block attempts to disable security tools or tamper with logging mechanisms, actions that ransomware actors often perform to evade detection or delay response.

For organizations that have integrated EDR with a broader orchestration and automation framework, automated playbooks can significantly reduce response times during a ransomware attack. When an alert is triggered indicating potential encryption behavior, the EDR system can automatically isolate the affected endpoint, collect relevant logs, alert security staff, and initiate forensic imaging. This automation reduces reliance on manual intervention during high-stress incidents and ensures that containment occurs quickly and consistently. These automated actions can be customized based on the severity of the threat, the sensitivity of the affected systems, or the confidence level of the detection.

EDR solutions are also instrumental in post-incident investigation and recovery. After a ransomware event, it is essential to understand the initial point of compromise, how the attacker moved through the environment, what data may have been accessed or exfiltrated, and whether any backdoors were left behind. The historical telemetry collected by EDR tools provides a timeline of events that helps incident response teams reconstruct the attack. This forensic capability supports root cause analysis, helps ensure that all artifacts are removed, and provides documentation for legal or regulatory obligations. It also informs future defensive strategies by revealing which controls failed and which detection rules need to be updated or expanded.

Ransomware threat actors increasingly engage in double extortion, where they exfiltrate data before encrypting systems and threaten to leak it publicly unless a ransom is paid. EDR platforms that monitor network connections and data transfer behavior can help detect these exfiltration activities. Large outbound data transfers, especially to unfamiliar IP addresses or through unapproved protocols, can be flagged and investigated before encryption is launched. This capability gives defenders a chance to act before attackers complete the most damaging phase of their operation.

Training and preparedness also factor into the successful use of EDR in ransomware mitigation. Security teams must be trained not only in how to use the EDR platform but in how to recognize early indicators of ransomware and respond decisively. Regular exercises, tabletop simulations, and red team assessments can expose weaknesses in detection rules, gaps in response procedures, or confusion in escalation paths. These findings can be used to refine EDR configurations, optimize playbooks, and improve coordination across the incident response team.

A comprehensive ransomware defense strategy supported by EDR also involves integration with backup and recovery systems. While EDR tools aim to prevent or contain attacks, it is crucial to prepare for worst-case scenarios where some systems are encrypted before detection occurs. EDR tools can assist recovery efforts by identifying exactly which files were encrypted, when, and by what process. This level of detail allows backup systems to target specific restoration points and avoid reintroducing compromised files. It also helps verify the integrity of restored systems by comparing pre-attack and post-attack configurations.

In a threat landscape dominated by ransomware groups that adapt quickly and strike without warning, EDR platforms provide defenders with a dynamic, intelligence-driven toolkit. Their ability to monitor activity at the endpoint level, detect early signs of attack, and respond in real time is essential for disrupting ransomware before it causes catastrophic damage. The effectiveness of EDR depends not only on its technical capabilities but on how it is operationalized—how well teams are trained, how thoroughly detection logic is maintained, and how seamlessly response actions are integrated into the broader security framework. As ransomware actors continue to innovate, so too must defenders leverage the full potential of EDR to build a defense posture that is both proactive and resilient.

Leveraging Open Source Tools in EDR

Open source tools have become indispensable in the cybersecurity ecosystem, and their role in enhancing Endpoint Detection and Response capabilities continues to grow. Organizations facing increasingly complex threat landscapes must often balance performance and flexibility with budgetary constraints. Open source tools offer a compelling solution, providing transparency, adaptability, and community-driven innovation without the high costs typically associated with commercial EDR products. While open source tools alone may not always replace a full-featured enterprise EDR suite, they serve as critical building blocks in constructing tailored, responsive, and cost-effective endpoint defense strategies. By integrating these tools into existing workflows, security teams can extend visibility, improve detection fidelity, and gain better control over endpoint behaviors in ways that align with their specific operational needs.

A fundamental advantage of open source tools in EDR is the visibility and control they provide. Unlike proprietary software, which often limits customization or obscures internal workings, open source tools allow security practitioners to inspect the source code, audit functionality, and modify behavior according to their environment. This transparency is especially valuable in a field where trust and assurance are paramount. Security teams can ensure that data is processed securely, telemetry is collected ethically, and backdoors or hidden vulnerabilities are not present. Moreover, open source communities are typically fast to react to new threats, with contributors updating detection rules, signatures, and behavioral indicators in response to emerging attack vectors.

One of the most widely used open source tools in EDR is OSQuery, originally developed by Facebook. OSQuery turns the operating system into a relational database, allowing administrators to write SQL-like queries to extract endpoint information. It supports Windows, macOS, and Linux, making it a flexible solution for heterogeneous environments. With OSQuery, analysts can monitor running processes, logged-in users, network connections, file changes, registry keys, and much more. Because it can be deployed in real time or on a scheduled basis, OSQuery is equally useful for proactive hunting and reactive investigation. Its integration with log management and SIEM tools enables seamless enrichment of alerts and the creation of custom detection logic that matches specific threat patterns observed in the organization.

Another valuable open source project is Velociraptor, which offers endpoint visibility, live forensic collection, and hunting capabilities. Velociraptor provides a scalable and powerful interface for querying endpoints, enabling security teams to collect volatile data, execute scripts, and perform memory analysis without interrupting system performance. It supports complex queries across large environments and includes a built-in artifact framework for defining reusable forensic workflows. Velociraptor's capabilities are especially useful during active incident response, where rapid triage of potentially compromised systems is required. Its ability to conduct targeted investigations without relying on full disk imaging or physical access accelerates decision-making and reduces time to containment.

Sigma, another prominent open source initiative, acts as a universal signature format for writing detection rules. While Sigma is not an EDR tool by itself, it allows analysts to express detection logic in a vendor-agnostic format that can be converted into queries for various platforms, including SIEMs and EDR tools. This interoperability makes Sigma an effective bridge between open source detection development and proprietary environments. Organizations can use Sigma to maintain a centralized, transparent repository of detection logic that evolves with the threat landscape and can be easily shared across platforms. Coupled with regular threat intelligence feeds, Sigma rules empower teams to build custom alerts tailored to the specific behaviors and attack techniques relevant to their environment.

For collecting and analyzing logs from endpoints, tools such as Sysmon and Winlogbeat play a significant role. Sysmon, developed by Microsoft, provides detailed logging of system activity, including process creation, network connections, and driver loading. When configured correctly, Sysmon offers a rich source of telemetry that rivals many commercial EDR solutions in granularity. Logs generated by Sysmon can be ingested into Elasticsearch via Winlogbeat, where they can be visualized, searched, and analyzed using the open source Elastic Stack. This combination allows for the creation of high-performance, low-cost detection and investigation platforms that can scale across thousands of endpoints.

While open source tools offer immense value, their integration and maintenance require dedicated effort. Unlike commercial solutions that often include user-friendly dashboards, support, and automated updates, open source EDR stacks demand configuration, scripting, and monitoring to function effectively. Organizations must invest time in building and documenting workflows, ensuring compatibility between tools, and training staff to use each component proficiently. Security teams must also stay engaged with the respective open source communities to track updates, report bugs, and contribute improvements. These efforts are well worth the outcome, as they result in a highly customizable, transparent, and responsive security posture that can be continuously evolved.

Open source EDR tools also encourage a mindset of collaboration and shared defense. Many cybersecurity teams contribute back to the tools they use, sharing detection rules, analysis scripts, and case studies that help others defend against similar threats. This community-driven model accelerates innovation and strengthens global cyber resilience. Whether through GitHub repositories, discussion forums, or threat research publications, practitioners engaged in the open source ecosystem are part of a broader movement that values accessibility, adaptability, and collective improvement.

In addition to technical capabilities, open source tools can also be aligned with broader strategic goals such as compliance and governance. Many regulatory frameworks require transparency in how security data is collected, stored, and processed. Open source tools facilitate this transparency, allowing organizations to demonstrate compliance through documented configurations, verifiable code, and audit-friendly logs. This is particularly important in industries where data sensitivity and regulatory scrutiny are high, such as healthcare, finance, and government. By leveraging open source tools, these organizations can ensure not only strong technical defenses but also accountability and verifiability in their security operations.

The decision to use open source tools in EDR is not just about cost savings, although the financial benefits are significant. It is about empowerment, flexibility, and control. It allows organizations to tailor their defenses to their specific risk profile, integrate with existing infrastructure, and respond to new threats without waiting for vendor roadmaps. As cyber threats continue to evolve, the ability to adapt quickly and innovate internally becomes a competitive advantage. Open source tools provide the foundation for building that advantage, offering a path toward more resilient, agile, and intelligent endpoint defense systems that can grow and evolve alongside the threats they are designed to counter. By strategically combining these tools, organizations can build a robust EDR capability that reflects their unique environment and strengthens their overall security posture.

Challenges of EDR in High-Availability Environments

Deploying and maintaining Endpoint Detection and Response solutions in high-availability environments presents a unique set of challenges that extend far beyond standard EDR implementation. High-availability environments are built to ensure continuous uptime, fault tolerance, and failover resilience for critical systems that must operate without interruption. These environments often span financial trading platforms, healthcare infrastructure, airline reservation systems, industrial control networks, and other mission-critical sectors where any downtime could result in significant financial loss, operational disruption, or risk to human life. While EDR platforms offer essential protection against modern threats, integrating them into such sensitive ecosystems requires careful planning, rigorous testing, and a deep understanding of the operational constraints involved.

One of the primary challenges is balancing security with performance. EDR tools operate by continuously monitoring system behavior, collecting telemetry, scanning files, intercepting process creation, and potentially injecting code into running applications to observe their activity. In environments where latency and performance are paramount, even the slightest degradation caused by background monitoring can be unacceptable. Financial trading systems, for example, operate on microsecond-level timing, and any delay introduced by EDR agents could disrupt transactions or trigger cascading system errors. Similarly, real-time data acquisition systems in industrial environments must maintain precise timing to ensure safety and accuracy. In such scenarios, EDR agents must be configured to operate in a minimal-impact mode or selectively disabled on endpoints where their performance footprint cannot be tolerated.

Another significant challenge lies in the complexity and diversity of systems typically found in high-availability environments. These systems often include a mix of legacy infrastructure, custom-built applications, and specialized hardware with proprietary operating systems. EDR platforms are usually designed for general-purpose endpoints like Windows, macOS, and Linux workstations or servers. Integrating them into nonstandard systems requires customized deployment procedures, manual tuning, and in some cases, complete exclusion of certain devices from monitoring. This lack of uniform coverage creates visibility gaps that adversaries can exploit. Moreover, EDR agents may be incompatible with critical applications, leading to system crashes or unpredictable behavior if not thoroughly tested. Ensuring compatibility without compromising the integrity of essential services is a constant balancing act.

Operational constraints also make change management particularly difficult in high-availability environments. EDR tools frequently require updates to agents, detection rules, and response policies to stay effective against evolving threats. However, applying these updates requires scheduled maintenance windows, rigorous testing, and stakeholder approvals, all of which are difficult to coordinate in environments that are designed to avoid downtime. The fear of introducing instability often leads organizations to delay updates, resulting in outdated or incomplete protection. In such cases, security teams must work closely with operations teams to create deployment pipelines that allow safe and efficient updates while preserving uptime and performance standards.

Incident response presents another layer of difficulty. In most EDR implementations, containment actions such as isolating endpoints, terminating processes, or quarantining files are central to stopping threats. In a high-availability context, these actions can have unintended consequences. Isolating a production server could disrupt core services for thousands of users. Terminating a process may interrupt a live transaction or corrupt a data stream. Therefore, response policies must be designed with surgical precision, often requiring extensive whitelisting, context-aware decision-making, and manual intervention. Automated responses, while useful in traditional environments, can pose a risk in systems where availability is more critical than the speed of containment. This reality forces incident responders to operate with heightened caution, often delaying containment in favor of deeper investigation, which can give threats more time to spread.

Logging and telemetry generation must also be handled differently in high-availability environments. While EDR platforms depend on collecting and transmitting large volumes of data to provide insight and support detection, this constant flow of information can strain bandwidth and processing resources. In environments where network performance is tightly controlled, excessive telemetry can impact operational traffic or exceed allowed limits for logging infrastructure. Furthermore, storing this data securely and ensuring its availability for analysis during an incident becomes a challenge when high-volume logs are generated across thousands of endpoints. Efficient log filtering, tiered retention policies, and integration with high-performance storage systems are required to avoid data overload while still maintaining investigative depth.

Interoperability with existing high-availability architectures is another critical concern. Many EDR platforms rely on central management consoles that must be highly available themselves. If these consoles experience downtime or performance degradation, it could hinder alerting, response, or configuration changes during an active threat. In high-availability environments, the EDR management infrastructure must be as fault-tolerant as the systems it protects, often requiring redundancy, failover clustering, and real-time synchronization between instances. This increases architectural complexity and demands close collaboration between security architects, infrastructure engineers, and application owners to ensure seamless integration.

Cultural and organizational barriers also play a role. In high-availability environments, the primary focus of operational teams is maintaining uptime and service continuity. Security is important, but it is often viewed through the lens of risk to availability rather than risk to confidentiality or integrity. This difference in priorities can lead to friction between security and operations teams, especially when proposed security measures are perceived as disruptive. Building a culture of collaboration, mutual understanding, and shared responsibility is essential to overcoming this barrier. Security teams must be prepared to communicate the value of EDR in terms that resonate with business and operational stakeholders, highlighting how improved detection and faster response can ultimately protect availability rather than threaten it.

Lastly, compliance and regulatory considerations must be carefully navigated. High-availability systems often operate in heavily regulated industries where data sovereignty, privacy laws, and audit requirements dictate how data can be collected, stored, and transmitted. EDR tools must be configured to comply with these regulations without compromising their effectiveness. This may involve anonymizing certain telemetry, storing data locally, or limiting the use of automated analysis tools that transfer data to the cloud. Meeting these requirements adds further complexity to deployment and ongoing management but is essential for maintaining regulatory alignment and avoiding legal or reputational repercussions.

Successfully implementing EDR in high-availability environments requires a tailored approach that respects the constraints of the systems being protected while still delivering the critical benefits of visibility, detection, and response. It involves technical precision, operational awareness, and cross-functional collaboration. EDR cannot be a one-size-fits-all solution in these settings. Instead, it must be designed as part of a broader security strategy that acknowledges the unique demands of continuous availability and integrates seamlessly with the existing ecosystem. Through careful planning, rigorous testing, and adaptive policy enforcement, organizations can achieve a balance between security and stability, ensuring that even their most sensitive and mission-critical systems are equipped to withstand today's advanced threats.

Future Trends in Endpoint Detection and Response

The future of Endpoint Detection and Response is rapidly taking shape in response to a constantly evolving threat landscape, technological innovation, and changing organizational needs. As cyberattacks become more sophisticated, stealthy, and targeted, the demands placed on EDR solutions are increasing significantly. Future EDR platforms will not only be required to detect known and unknown threats in real time but also to do so across a growing array of devices, environments, and usage patterns. This expansion is pushing the boundaries of what EDR systems must accomplish, and several critical trends are emerging that will define the future trajectory of endpoint security.

One of the most transformative trends in EDR is the convergence with other security technologies into unified platforms. Historically, endpoint protection, detection and response, threat intelligence, and security orchestration tools have operated as separate systems with limited integration. Going forward, organizations are seeking tighter consolidation that offers seamless workflows, shared telemetry, and centralized visibility. The integration of EDR with extended detection and response platforms, known as XDR, is a natural evolution. XDR expands EDR's capabilities by collecting and correlating telemetry not only from endpoints but also from cloud workloads, identity systems, email gateways, and network traffic. By aggregating data from multiple sources, XDR enables earlier and more precise threat detection, improved context, and more effective automated responses. EDR will increasingly serve as the foundational component of this broader ecosystem.

Artificial intelligence and machine learning are also playing a larger role in the evolution of EDR capabilities. While many EDR platforms already leverage basic machine learning models to identify anomalies, future implementations will feature far more advanced algorithms capable of continuously learning from global threat data, adapting to specific organizational behaviors, and reducing the reliance on static rules. These models will not only enhance detection but also prioritize alerts based on potential impact, analyze root cause, and even suggest or execute response actions. The move toward predictive analytics will allow security teams to preemptively detect signs of compromise before any observable damage occurs, based on subtle shifts in user or process behavior that might otherwise go unnoticed.

Automation and orchestration are also becoming essential to the future of EDR. As the volume of alerts and the sophistication of attacks grow, manual response processes are proving inadequate. Security teams often face alert fatigue, resource limitations, and the challenge of acting quickly enough to prevent threat escalation. Future EDR systems will integrate with automated playbooks capable of investigating alerts, validating incidents, and executing containment actions without requiring human intervention for every step. These automated workflows will be dynamic, adapting based on context such as asset criticality, threat severity, or user role. As EDR tools become more autonomous, the role of human analysts will shift toward oversight, strategy, and incident analysis, rather than performing repetitive triage tasks.

Another emerging trend is the expansion of EDR coverage beyond traditional endpoints. The definition of an endpoint is evolving to include mobile devices, IoT sensors, industrial control systems, and edge computing nodes. As enterprises embrace digital transformation, cloud-native applications, and hybrid infrastructures, the attack surface has expanded dramatically. Future EDR platforms must be designed to monitor and protect these diverse environments without compromising performance or usability. Lightweight agents, agentless monitoring techniques, and API integrations will become more common as organizations seek to extend EDR visibility across all parts of their infrastructure, regardless of device type or operating environment.

Cloud-based EDR is gaining traction as organizations seek scalable, flexible, and globally available solutions. Rather than relying on on-premises management servers, cloud-native EDR platforms offer real-time telemetry analysis, global threat intelligence integration, and centralized policy management from any location. This model is particularly appealing for distributed enterprises, remote workforces, and organizations looking to simplify deployment and maintenance. However, it also introduces challenges related to data sovereignty, compliance, and latency, which future EDR providers will need to address with innovative architectures that combine local execution with cloud intelligence in a hybrid model.

The emphasis on privacy and regulatory compliance will shape the evolution of EDR as well. With stricter laws governing personal data, employee monitoring, and cross-border data flows, future EDR solutions will need to strike a balance between security and privacy. This may involve anonymizing certain telemetry, providing transparency about data collection practices, and allowing customizable levels of data visibility based on user roles or jurisdictional requirements. EDR systems that can deliver strong security outcomes without overstepping privacy boundaries will become more attractive, especially in sectors such as healthcare, finance, and government.

The role of user and entity behavior analytics will become increasingly central in EDR platforms. By building comprehensive behavior baselines for individual users, devices, and applications, EDR tools can detect deviations that indicate insider threats, compromised accounts, or malicious use of legitimate tools. These analytics will be powered by real-time data and enriched with contextual information such as time, location, and historical activity. As threats become more evasive and blend into normal operations, this behavioral context will be critical in distinguishing harmless anomalies from serious threats.

Future EDR systems will also place greater emphasis on collaboration and shared defense. As cyber threats become more global and state-sponsored attacks increase in frequency, the ability to share threat intelligence across organizations and sectors will be vital. EDR platforms will support secure threat sharing protocols, standardized indicator formats, and integration with national and international security initiatives. Organizations will be able to benefit from crowd-sourced intelligence, community-driven detection rules, and coordinated response strategies, helping to close detection gaps and improve defensive capabilities for everyone involved.

Education and accessibility will play a major role in the democratization of EDR technology. While large enterprises have the resources to deploy and manage complex security platforms, small and medium-sized organizations often struggle with budget and staffing limitations. Future EDR tools will need to be more intuitive, with simplified user interfaces, prebuilt detection content, and automated configurations that allow even small teams to benefit from advanced protection. Vendors will focus on reducing the barrier to entry by offering subscription models, managed services, and educational resources that help organizations of all sizes build effective endpoint defense strategies.

In addition to all these developments, the continued evolution of threat actors will keep shaping the direction of EDR technology. Adversaries are already using artificial intelligence to evade detection, automate attacks, and develop polymorphic malware. In response, defenders must use similarly advanced techniques to detect and respond at machine speed. EDR platforms will need to anticipate and adapt to these innovations with equally advanced defenses, leveraging large-scale behavioral datasets, threat intelligence correlation, and autonomous response capabilities to stay ahead of attackers.

As the cybersecurity landscape becomes more complex, the future of EDR will depend on its ability to evolve beyond traditional endpoint monitoring into an intelligent, integrated, and adaptive platform that supports the entire security lifecycle. The convergence of machine learning, automation, cross-platform visibility, and behavioral context will redefine how threats are detected, analyzed, and neutralized. The organizations that embrace these changes and invest in next-generation EDR solutions will be better equipped to safeguard their assets, protect their users, and ensure operational continuity in a world where the endpoint is often the first and last line of defense.

Strategic Roadmap for EDR Maturity

Developing a mature Endpoint Detection and Response program requires a structured and strategic approach that aligns technology, processes, and people to the evolving threat landscape and organizational priorities. EDR maturity is not achieved by simply deploying a toolset. It is the result of deliberate planning, iterative improvement, cross-functional coordination, and the integration of detection and response into the broader security operations framework. A strategic roadmap provides the necessary guidance to transition from a basic or reactive deployment to a fully integrated, proactive, and intelligent EDR capability that supports the resilience and agility of the organization.

The journey toward EDR maturity begins with establishing foundational visibility across all relevant endpoints. In the initial stages, organizations often focus on deploying EDR agents to the most critical systems, such as domain controllers, file servers, and high-value endpoints. However, to reach operational effectiveness, this coverage must expand to include the entire endpoint landscape, including laptops, workstations, cloud-hosted workloads, mobile devices, and any asset that processes or stores sensitive data. Ensuring comprehensive and consistent deployment is essential for creating a baseline of activity and detecting lateral movement or suspicious behavior early in the attack chain. At this stage, organizations should prioritize building asset inventories and identifying unmanaged endpoints, as visibility gaps undermine the effectiveness of EDR analytics.

Once deployment is stabilized, the next step is to establish detection logic tailored to the organization's unique environment. EDR platforms typically come with out-of-the-box rulesets, but these are often generic and may generate high volumes of false positives or miss context-specific threats. Security teams must begin the process of detection tuning by analyzing alerts, suppressing known benign behaviors, and creating custom rules that reflect the operational realities of the business. This process requires close collaboration between security analysts, IT administrators, and business unit leaders to understand what constitutes normal behavior, what activities should be flagged, and how to contextualize alerts. Detection engineering becomes a core capability at this stage, requiring the development of detection content, documentation standards, and mechanisms for ongoing validation.

With effective detection in place, attention turns to response. EDR maturity involves not just identifying threats but responding to them efficiently and appropriately. This requires the development and refinement of response playbooks that define how various incident types should be handled. These playbooks must address containment, remediation, communication, and escalation procedures. At early stages, response actions may be largely manual, depending on analysts to review alerts and execute tasks through the EDR console. Over time, automation should be introduced to handle repetitive and time-sensitive actions such as isolating endpoints, killing malicious processes, or collecting forensic snapshots. Mature organizations create tiered response plans that escalate based on severity, ensuring that incidents are triaged and managed according to risk and impact.

Metrics and measurement are critical for tracking progress along the roadmap. Organizations must define key performance indicators that reflect their detection and response capabilities. These may include mean time to detect, mean time to contain, alert-to-incident conversion rates, or false positive ratios. By collecting and analyzing these metrics over time, security leaders can identify areas of improvement, justify resource investments, and demonstrate the value of EDR to executive stakeholders. Regular reviews of these metrics should be integrated into security governance processes, with findings feeding directly into roadmap updates and operational adjustments.

As EDR operations mature, organizations should begin to shift from reactive incident response to proactive threat hunting. Threat hunting involves the manual or semi-automated exploration of EDR data to uncover indicators of compromise that may have evaded existing detection logic. This capability requires skilled analysts who are familiar with adversary tactics, techniques, and procedures, and who can construct hypotheses, query endpoint telemetry, and pivot across data sources to validate or refute their theories. Threat hunting not only uncovers hidden threats but also informs improvements to detection rules and enhances the organization's understanding of its threat landscape. Mature programs operationalize hunting through scheduled hunts, hunt documentation, and integration with red and blue team exercises.

Integration is another major milestone on the path to EDR maturity. EDR tools must not operate in isolation but instead must be part of a larger ecosystem of security technologies, including SIEMs, SOAR platforms, identity and access management systems, and threat intelligence platforms. Integration enables richer alert enrichment, cross-platform correlation, automated response workflows, and better situational awareness. Organizations should invest in API-based integrations, data normalization, and workflow orchestration to ensure that EDR data can be used effectively across the security stack. Mature EDR programs contribute telemetry and insights to broader security analytics, supporting enterprise-wide threat detection and response.

Training and workforce development are also fundamental to EDR maturity. Analysts must be trained not only in the technical use of the EDR platform but also in broader areas such as digital forensics, malware analysis, and adversary emulation. Organizations should establish formal training plans, encourage certifications, and provide access to threat intelligence resources and lab environments. Peer learning, knowledge sharing, and internal documentation help to institutionalize expertise and reduce reliance on individual contributors. As the team matures, roles may become more specialized, with dedicated detection engineers, threat hunters, and incident responders working together under a unified operational model.

Governance and strategic alignment represent the final stage of EDR maturity. At this level, EDR becomes an embedded part of organizational risk management and decision-making. Security leadership uses EDR insights to inform board-level discussions, regulatory compliance strategies, and long-term technology planning. The EDR roadmap itself becomes a living document, regularly reviewed and updated to reflect changes in business priorities, threat intelligence, and emerging technologies. Strategic investments are made in line with the roadmap, ensuring that the EDR program continues to evolve and remain aligned with both internal requirements and external threats.

A mature EDR program does not exist in a vacuum. It is supported by a culture of continuous improvement, operational excellence, and strategic foresight. Organizations that follow a deliberate and structured roadmap can transform their EDR deployment from a reactive tool into a proactive, intelligent system that supports business resilience, reduces risk, and enhances security posture in measurable and meaningful ways. Through careful planning, consistent execution, and adaptive learning, the journey toward EDR maturity becomes not only achievable but sustainable, enabling organizations to meet today's challenges and anticipate tomorrow's threats with confidence.